Acknowledgments

We would like to thank the following people:

Sally Long, for encouragement, help, and support.
Terry Johnson and the staff at Mayer-Johnson.
Helene Prokesch and Margaret Deavours at Lekotek of Georgia.
Students, past and present, at Fulton County Schools in Atlanta, Georgia.

And lastly, our families—we love you!

About the Authors

Jane Kelly, Speech and Language Pathologist

Jane Kelly received her M.Ed. from Georgia State University and her M.M.Sc. degree in Speech/Language Pathology from Emory University. She is currently working as a Speech Therapist in Fulton County Public Schools and is a Lekotek Leader with Lekotek of Georgia. Ms. Kelly has 13 years of experience working with multihandicapped students, many of whom are non-verbal.

Teresa Friend, Augmentative Communication Specialist

Teresa Friend is an Augmentative Communication Specialist with the Fulton County system in Atlanta, Ga. She received her M.S. in Speech/Language Pathology from Georgia State University. Ms. Friend has spent 13 years working with nonverbal students and is now in charge of assessing and evaluating student communication needs for the county.

Contents

Seasons of the Year Unit 269

Book Resources 359

Additional Resources 362

Literature List 363

AUTHOR'S NOTE:
The books selected for More Hands-on Reading were available at our school library. Since the first printing of the book, some of these books have gone out of print and may be more difficult to find (Easter Parade and Clean House for Mole and Mouse). If you cannot find a title at your local or school library, try small book stores or used book stores. If the book still cannot be found, subsitute a similar book with the same topic and customize the activities and overlays for the new story.

Introduction

Introduction

Rationale

*M*ore Hands-on Reading is a continuation of *Hands-on Reading*, an instructional resource book which uses popular children's literature as a vehicle for teaching using a whole-language approach.

All children, regardless of ability, need and benefit from exposure to written language and reading experiences. Therefore, we have developed resource materials as a guide to making classic children's literature more accessible to special needs students. A unique goal of the Hands-on Reading program is to maximize the participation of nonverbal children in interactive storytime activities through the use of various augmentative communication strategies.

More Hands-on Reading IS:

- A whole-language resource book.
- A way to share literature successfully with special needs students and their peers.
- An introduction to reading readiness.
- A means to promote emergent literacy skills.
- A menu of suggested books and activities to pick and choose from.
- Teacher-friendly with quick and easy creative ideas.
- Easy and fun to implement.
- Adaptable.
- Reproducible for classroom use.
- A total communication approach to language.

More Hands-on Reading Is NOT:

- A traditional reading program.
- A recipe book that must be followed precisely and in its entirety.
- A phonics program.
- An academic curriculum.
- All inclusive.
- A guide to Augmentative Communication.
- Difficult.

Overview

" Each unit offers I.E.P. goals and objectives, music, computer, and literature resources."

*M*ore Hands-on Reading presents a selection of 16 classic children's books that have been grouped into three thematic units:

- ■ Holidays

- ■ Seasons of the Year

- ■ Family Fun

Each thematic unit offers I.E.P. goals and objectives and lists music, computer, and related literature resources. Each book selection within a thematic unit includes a plot summary followed by suggested hands-on activities: music, props, art, cooking, literacy, and carryover. In addition, there are corresponding communication overlays. Through the adaptive strategies outlined in these sections, some level of participation is ensured for all children.

How to use this book

" It is not necessary to use every storybook included in this resource guide to be successful. "

When beginning a thematic unit, choose more than one book to read. It is not necessary to use every storybook included in this resource guide to be successful. It is also possible to substitute books of similar theme or content.

The suggested activities can easily be used with other storybooks if minor adaptations are made. Establish continuity when doing hands-on activities by always starting with the book. Read the story before each activity to make the book's language and concepts come alive.

The following are suggestions for successfully implementing a whole-language program utilizing this resource book.

Sharing the Story

" For large groups we highly recommend Big Books."

Try to seat your group so that illustrations can be easily seen. For a small group, a semicircle on the floor works well. For large groups, we highly recommend choosing stories that are available in Big Book format. When reading, feel free to adjust the text to suit your audience (simplifying complex sentence forms, adapting vocabulary, etc.).

The storybooks should be read more than once over a several day period. Involve students by using props (see below) and having them turn pages, act out parts, and speak lines. You may want to let young children come up and touch a picture on the page. Leave the books out on the shelf for independent student browsing.

Using Props During Story Time

"Props transform children from passive listeners to active learners."

We strongly recommend the use of props during storytime. They add the element of play that transforms children from passive listeners to active learners.

Props can be anything from real items such as objects, toys, stuffed animals, or puppets, to photographs, pictures, or symbol cards. Battery operated toys are ideal and can be adapted easily for switch users (see page 14). When children have an opportunity to manipulate a prop during storytime, a crucial link from the abstract (the printed word) to the concrete is provided.

Assemble props before the reading of the story. For example, for *Goodnight, Moon* obtain a bunny rabbit and some of the household items that occur in the story. Let each child choose a prop to hold. Puppets can talk, clothes can be put on, food can be eaten — the role-playing possibilities are endless.

Props can make the difference between a successful storytime experience and one that falls flat. Children can hold a toy. A toy can also "hold" a child.

Art

Art activities are included for each storybook. Art experiences are ideal for incorporating choice making (such as choosing colors), making requests (asking for needed tools and materials), and reinforcing new vocabulary. Art activities are concrete, manipulative, and at the same time language rich. If our goal is to take words and make them real, art activities are a must.

Traditional art supplies (paint brushes, crayons, scissors, etc.) don't work for every student. Many easy adaptations can be made by the teacher or with the help of an occupational therapist. Crayons and paint brushes can be built up or adapted handles made. Try using Velcro® straps to enable a child to hold an implement independently. If standard paint brushes are too small, try large-size brushes or small paint rollers. The key is adapting the activity so the child, not the teacher, is the artist.

For children with severe motor impairments, stamp art provides a means for creative but accessible artistic expression. The classic method is an old standby—potato printing. Craft stores sell a pop-up sponge that can be easily cut into a variety of shapes—when wet, the sponge expands. The sponge form can be dipped by hand into tempera paint or hot-glued to a block or other mounting material. "Fun foam" is also sold in craft stores. It is thin enough to cut with the standard letter and shape cutters that are found in many schools and teacher centers. The foam stamp is then hot glued to a mount and a handle added if required. These adapted stamps can then be used to make pictures or illustrate a story.

Music

Music is definitely a "must-do" for any whole-language classroom. We know of no better way to promote student engagement than through music. It brings a group together, captures attention, and turns excess energy into something fun. Starting storytime with music sets the stage for a pleasurable event.

There are many wonderful sources for recorded music listed in the resource section of each unit. Recorded music has an advantage of being loud, rhythmic, and fun to follow. It is easy to involve nonverbal students or switch users by plugging in the record or tape player into an environmental control unit (ECU). Attach the switch to the ECU, and the switch user is now in charge of turning the music on and off.

Many augmentative communication devices can enable nonverbal students to "sing." It is especially simple to program a song into AC devices with digitized (recorded) speech, such as the MACAW. For WOLF users, it may be more practical to program repeated lines (e-i-e-i-o) or major vocabulary items (cow, pig, etc.) to be interjected into the song.

Occasionally it's hard to find a song that exactly suits your story. Try making up your own lyrics, and setting them to a familiar tune. Familiar tunes include:

♪ London Bridge

♪ Mary Had a Little Lamb

♪ Here We Go Round the Mulberry Bush

♪ Did You Ever See a Lassie?

♪ Frere Jacques

♪ Twinkle, Twinkle Little Star

♪ The Farmer in the Dell

♪ Row, Row, Row Your Boat

With props or pictures to supplement the words, children can learn your made-up masterpiece surprisingly fast. Or even help compose it!

Cooking

As with art, cooking provides rich opportunities for language use in a meaningful context. To cook (something edible!) students must locate or request the appropriate ingredients and follow a recipe in the correct sequence. And, of course, students receive a tangible reward for their efforts — good food.

Many of the cooking activities can be adapted for switch users by obtaining an environmental control unit. These devices provide a switch interface for electrical appliances. A blender, electric mixer, or any other appliance can be turned on and off by the switch. This enables a physically disabled student to control many parts of the cooking process.

Overlays are included for most cooking activities. In many cases, these overlays can also double as a printed recipe. For more complex recipes, recipe strips are provided. These strips give the recipe in symbol sentence form. They can be used simply as directions to be read and followed. They can also be used in sequencing activities, and the sentence strips cut, assembled, and stapled along the left edge to create a make-and-take book.

To enable a switch user to read a recipe to the class in sequence, refer to the Augmentative Communication section of this introduction for directions in programming the "list" command on the WOLF page 10.

Literacy and Carryover Activities

Literacy Activities

The literacy activities were developed as a means to provide reading opportunities for students. All children love to read out loud. *More Hands-on Reading* includes many make-and-take books, peek-a-boo pictures, sequence books, and cut-and-paste picture pages, which are designed to complement the text of the story. After reading the literature selection, create these literacy projects with your students. Symbol sentences are included on each page. The teacher or student can point to the symbols as the sentences are read. To encourage successful student reading, the symbol sentences are laid out on the page from left to right, and the symbols are paired with text. The Picture Communication Symbols are boxed to provide maximum visual impact. Adequate space between words is given to accommodate a pointing finger.

We have found that with minimal instruction, many students are able to read these make-and-take books out loud to teachers and friends. Binding them with construction paper creates a lasting library of books for the classroom. Sending these home allows the family to share in the fun.

Carryover Activities

Pencil and paper carryover activities are included for each storybook selection. These are optional and may be omitted if they do not suit your teaching style.

The "Tell Me About It" sheets may be used in an auditory scanning fashion for use with nonverbal students. When having a class discussion following the reading of a story, students can point to or mark their responses after the teacher has scanned through these out loud. They can also be used to reinforce vocabulary and concepts that occur in the storyline.

These sheets can also be useful in inclusion settings. When working in regular education classrooms, we have found that teachers almost without exception provide pencil and paper activities for their students. In order to have special needs students participate in normal class routines, we have adapted some worksheet activities for their use. Surprisingly, we found that our students loved them. Perhaps the desire to have an "A+" or a "100" written on top of your paper is universal to children!

Augmentative Communication

Augmentative Communication Device Overlays

The goal of *More Hands-on Reading* is to maximize student participation in whole language activities and specifically to increase opportunities for communication during literature lessons. Therefore, many strategies for augmentative communication have been included. The following section will review these strategies and offer suggestions for implementation.

Communication Overlays

" The overlays provided with each story were developed specifically for the story and not for everyday conversational needs."

The various communication overlays included in each story unit have been designed for use with the Macaw and the Wolf or Hawk. The overlays provided were developed specifically for storytime use and the suggested activities. They are not intended to be used as all-purpose communication boards for everyday conversational needs.

The first series of overlays in each unit corresponds to that literature selection. The easier grids are first (one and two location grids) and contain the repeated line or theme of that book. The following overlays are generally 8 or 9 location grids. Overlays are also provided for art, cooking, and music activities.

All of the overlays or displays can easily be adapted for use with other augmentative communication devices. Simply duplicate the overlay, cut out the desired picture symbols, and attach to a grid appropriate for your specific device. The overlays can also be used as communication boards without voice output.

How to make the Communication Overlays:

To use the story overlays:
1. Photocopy the desired overlay and color it.
2. Cut out the overlay to fit onto the device touch panel and laminate if desired.
3. Place the colored overlay onto the device touch panel. **NOTE:** You may need to tape the overlay onto the touch panel, so that it is aligned properly; e.g., Wolf/Hawk grids.

4. Program messages to correspond to the picture symbol locations on the overlay. You may choose to program complete sentences, phrases or single words; e.g., "The kitten was not his mother," rather than, "kitten," in *Are You My Mother?*

NOTE: Some overlays have specific programming instructions on the bottom of the page as well as suggested messages. See **Programming Tips**, page 14, in this section for additional device programming directions.

Programming Tips, page 14,

> **"** *Customize the communication displays to suit your student's needs.* **"**

We strongly encourage you to customize the communication displays to suit your student's needs and create your own. You may need to enlarge the symbols or reduce the number of symbols on a page. Some students may benefit more from concrete symbols such as objects or color photographs rather than picture communication symbols on a display.

For switch users, copy, cut out, and attach a picture communication symbol directly to their switch.

Experiment and enjoy! The "right" overlay is whichever one works for your student.

How to use the Communication Overlays:

> **"** *As you read the story, model use of the student's device.* **"**

After you have created your storytime overlay and programmed the messages, you might need to familiarize your students with the overlay layout and vocabulary items. As you read the story, model use of the device. Instead of speaking the repetitive line, you can activate the message on the device. Hold up a prop and have your students find the matching picture communication symbol on the overlay. Or students can choose a prop for storytelling by activating the symbol on the device. Students can retell the story, answer questions, or identify characters through pointing to the picture communication symbols.

Read the story numerous times over a 1-2 week period using the same communication display. Through repetition, the children will be able to predict the storyline sequence and access the overlay accurately.

Some overlays have been designed for exploratory play (*Corduroy's Christmas, Goodnight Moon, Easter Parade*), where students can independently explore an overlay and activate different locations to discover the hidden messages. Other overlays can be used to play a game (Simon Says, Hide & Seek). Several overlays have been included for use during the suggested art, cooking, and music activities.

Different prompts may be needed for different children. Some children may require a physical prompt/guide to access the appropriate symbol at first. Other students may benefit from a model or a verbal cue. A small penlight/flashlight can be held over the desired response to provide a visual cue.

The goal is to ensure success and participation as much as possible for all students.

Storyboards
Obtain a piece of foam-backed posterboard from an office supply store. Cut this board into the desired shape (a long piece about 5" wide works well). To this piece, attach a strip of sticky-back Velcro (the loop side) down the middle.

Mount desired picture communication symbols onto cards and attach a small square of hook Velcro to the back. These cards can now be stuck to the storyboard by the teacher or students.

Storyboards are useful in a variety of ways. They can serve as simple communication systems. During storytime, placing symbol cards can help sequence the story. They can be used as choice boards for students to choose props or other needed materials. During music activities, placing appropriate cards on the board can help teach the song and remember its sequence.

Alternative Communication Systems

The Wolf
The Wolf is a low-cost, voice-output communication device which features synthetic (robotic) speech. It has a large memory to store vocabulary pages in 3-user sections. The grids can be configured for 1-location messages up to 36-location messages. See Wolf Programming tips for special switch access features, page 14.

A.I.P.S. Wolf
The A.I.P.S. Wolf is a Mega Wolf with an attached switch unit with 9 jacks. Each jack can take one switch which, when activated, speaks one corresponding message. The touch panel of the A.I.P.S. Wolf can still be activated by direct selection. This AC device can meet the needs of two different users at

once: a switch user and a direct selection user. Character lines or song lyrics can be assigned to students by plugging their switch into the specific message. Change the message for a student by moving his/her switch to a different jack.

The Hawk

The Hawk is an inexpensive AC device which offers good recorded speech quality, limited memory, and easy/fast programming capabilities. The touch panel is divided into a 3x3 grid with each location allowing for up to 5 seconds of recorded speech for a total of 45 seconds.

The Hawk is ideal for fast programming of songs, related activities, and story lines. Therefore, many 3x3 location overlays have been included in this book.

The Macaw(s)

The family of Macaw communication devices feature light-weight devices with excellent recorded speech quality and extended amounts of memory. The Macaw can come with a variety of scanning modes, including auditory scanning for switch users.

"There are many inexpensive augmentative communication devices on the market for beginners."

Introductory AC systems

There are many inexpensive augmentative communication devices on the market for beginners. They typically feature a limited amount of memory for recorded speech (1-8 messages). They are lightweight, portable, and very easy to program. The devices we have successfully used in conjunction with literature lessons include:
- Cheap Talk
- Speakeasy
- Big Mac
- Talking Switch Plates

Environmental Control Units

Environmental control units are very useful in increasing classroom participation of students who require switch access. Attach any electrical appliance to the unit as well as a switch. When a student activates the switch, the appliance is turned on/off; e.g., lamps, Christmas tree lights, vacuum cleaners, etc. During music activities, plug a record player or tape recorder into the environmental control unit. By pressing the switch, students can control turning the music on and off (try playing musical chairs). A blender, food processor, mixer, or popcorn popper can be attached to an environmental control unit so switch users can participate in cooking activities also.

Battery Device Adapters

Battery device adapters allow you to make any battery-operated toy switch accessible. You simply place the copper disk of the battery adapter between the battery and the battery contact in the toy and close the battery compartment cover. You may need to remove part of the cover to allow the wire to fit through. Plug a switch into the battery device adapter and make sure the toy's control is set to "on." Now the toy can be operated through the switch. Battery-adapted toys make excellent interactive props for storytime.

See order information for all the AC materials listed in the Additional Resources section, page 362.

Programming Tips

All devices come with manuals for specific programming directions. The following section includes a few helpful hints.

Single Switch Access of Any Super or Mega Wolf

" The upper left corner square of any Wolf grid can be switch activated. "

The upper left corner square of any Wolf grid can be switch activated through the jack underneath the yellow sliding panel. Remove the yellow panel by pushing down firmly on the top two corners and sliding it down. Plug any 1/8" switch into the jack. Any message programmed into the upper left corner square of any page will be spoken when the switch is activated, once this function is turned on.

To turn on the switch access feature of the Wolf, follow these steps in order:

1. Turn on the Wolf.
2. Select "Trap" (press the top left location 0 and the top right location 30, simultaneously. Wolf says, "Trap, ___ page ___."
3. Select GO TO <u>ANY</u> SECTION <u>ANY</u> PAGE (square #2). Wolf says, "Choose section."
4. Select System Section, which is Section 1 (square #1). Wolf says, "Choose page."
5. Select System Page 4 (square #4). Wolf says, "System Page 4."
6. Select Switch In (square #14, 20). Wolf says, "Switch In."

WOW! You did it! If the Wolf is turned off, it will still keep the switch access function on. To deactivate the switch access, follow steps 1-5 above and then select "Normal In" (square #17,23).

Practical use

The switch access function is useful if you have a student who cannot directly select a message on the Wolf touch panel. You can program the repetitive line of the story or song in the upper left corner of a grid. Attach a corresponding picture communication symbol to a switch, plug it into the jack of the Wolf, and the student can activate the switch to "speak" the repetitive line. The touch panel of the Wolf is still available to other students, which is helpful for sharing the device.

Programming the List Command on a Wolf

" The list command speaks messages in sequential order."

The list command speaks messages from a programmed vocabulary page (data page) in sequential order, from the top of the page to the bottom. When a switch is attached to the jack under the yellow cover of the Wolf and the List Command is programmed, a student can tell a story, nursery rhyme, recite a recipe, or sing a song—all through switch activation!

You must be familiar with basic phonemic programming of the Wolf!
To program the list command follow these steps in order:

" You can program the repetitive line of the story or song in the upper left corner of a grid and attach a switch."

1. Set up a user page (data page), and program the messages you want spoken in order from top to bottom, left to right. (Remember the # of the user page you programmed this on; for this example we'll say user page 35.)
2. Set up a second user page and dimension it to be a 1x1 grid (on user page 34 for this example). You are on the Edit Page!
3. Select GOTO Command List Page (square #2 on the Edit Page, System p. 1). Wolf says, "Command List."
4. Select List (square #8) on the Command List Page, System p. 3, Wolf says,"List, choose Page."
5. Select the user page number that you programmed the messages on in step #1.
6. Select ASSIGN BUFFER, (square #31), Wolf says, "Assign."
7. Select anywhere on the Wolf touch panel.
8. Turn the Wolf Off.

Now, turn on the Wolf and select the 1x1 user page (34). The Wolf goes to the user page (35) where you programmed your messages and speaks them in sequence with each switch activation.

Practical Use

" Use the list command to allow students to speak items in sequence through simple switch activation."

You can program "Simon Says," recipes, nursery rhymes, the days of the week, the months of the year, numbers, the alphabet, or story lines of a book and then use the List Command to allow students to "speak" these items in sequence through simple switch activation. This can be a very powerful tool for switch users!

Programming Single Messages

Repetitive lines of a story or suggested song can be easily programmed on a Big Mac or Talking Switch. Record the single message into the device and then attach a picture communication symbol to the device/switch. Then students who are just beginning to use AC can actively participate in the literature lessons too.

Creating Your Own Literature Lessons

More Hands-On Reading certainly does not contain all of the possibilities for using literature lessons in the classroom. There are scores of excellent stories available in book stores, catalogs, and libraries that would generate wonderful learning experiences.We hope *More Hands-On Reading* will motivate teachers, therapists, and parents alike to create their own whole-language literature lessons for their special students.

" We hope MORE Hands-on Reading will motivate teachers to create their own whole-language literature lessons."

Planning a thematic unit with several book selections is easy and fun. First, you must decide on your thematic unit, which should come from your classroom curriculum or students' I.E.P.s. Then consult with a media specialist or librarian for available books on that topic and the appropriate age level desired. We recommend using Big Books whenever possible.

Once you have selected your books, you can use the Literature Lesson outline, page 18, to plan your activities for each story. Brainstorm with the other professionals (art, music teachers, speech therapists, occupational therapists, physical therapists, teacher assistants, librarian, etc.) working with your students, for creative, easy art projects, cooking ideas, songs, computer software, etc.

Assemble props to go along with the story. Communication overlays need to be developed to correspond to the story selection as well as any related activities. Use a team approach so all members have input as well as shared responsibilities for providing props, art/cooking supplies, and programming the communication displays. After you have planned your literature lesson and completed the outline, copy it and distribute it to all professionals involved.

" Read the same book for a 1-2 week period and teach a thematic unit for 1 to 1 1/2 months."

We suggest reading the same book for a 1-2 week period and teaching a thematic unit for a 1-1 1/2 month period.

Before each related activity (art, cooking, literacy, etc.), read the book selection so children can relate the activity back to the text; i.e., read *Are You My Mother?* and then make rice krispy birds' nests. Repetition of the story ensures increased comprehension and participation for all students.

It is always difficult to find planning time, yet careful, creative planning leads to successful learning experiences for both students and teachers.

Literature Lesson Outline

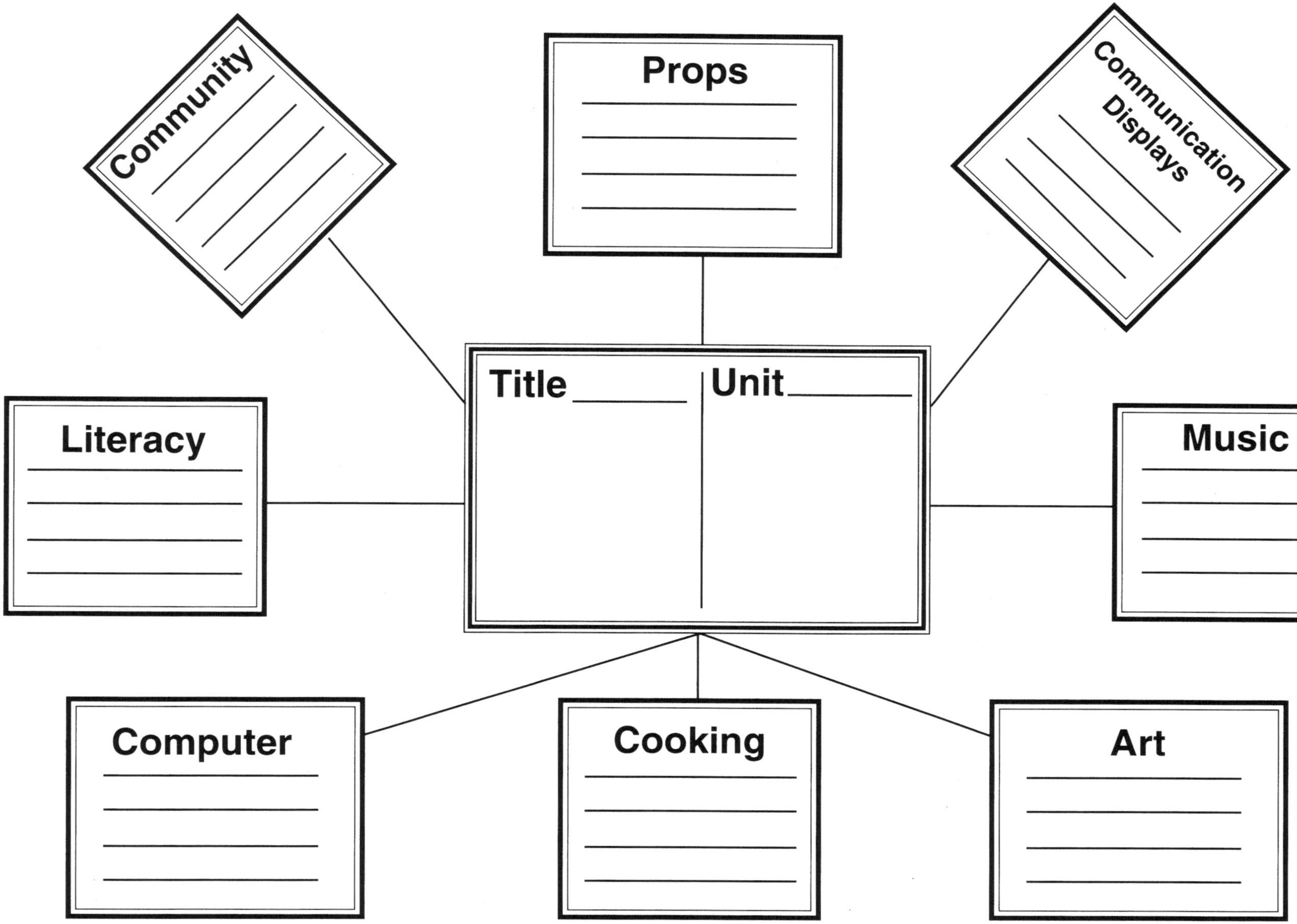

Computer

Literacy

Community

Title _____

Unit _____

Props

Cooking

Art

Music

Communication Displays

Interactive Reading Overlay - Wolf

Let's read a book!	Turn the page.	I can't see.
That's funny!	Uh-oh!	That's yucky!
My turn!	More!	What's that?

Interactive Reading Overlay - Macaw

Book Bulletin

Dear Parent,

We read _____

by _____ this week.

Our special hands-on project was:

Vocabulary we focused on includes:

Activities for home carryover:

Other stories to read at home:

Happy Reading!

Holiday Fun Unit

Holiday Unit

Introduction

In the world of children, time isn't measured by weeks and months. The child's year is marked by the progression of Halloween to Thanksgiving, and all the other magical times of secrets, surprises, and celebrations. The five books in this unit celebrate holidays. Holiday stories bring the excitement of the season alive and lend themselves to activities that are rich in language and opportunities for learning.

Holiday Unit

Literature Selections
See page 360 for book sources.
(Note: This unit can be completed using all or a portion of the books listed below.)

Big Pumpkin. Erica Silverman. Macmillan Publishing Co., New York.
ISBN: 0-68-980129-7

Over the River and Through the Wood. Lydia Maria Child. Illustrated by Nadine
Bernard Westcott., Harper Collins, New York.
ISBN: 0-06-021305-5

Corduroy's Christmas. Don Freeman.
ISBN: 0-67-084477-2

The Gingerbread Man. Traditional, Illustrated by Karen Lee Schmidt., Scholastic, Inc.,
New York.
ISBN: 0-590-41056-3

The Easter Parade. Mary Chalmers. Harper and Row., New York.
ISBN: 0-06-021232-2

I.E.P. Goals and Objectives

The child will:

☐ identify and express spatial concepts:
    ☐ in
    ☐ on
    ☐ under

☐ demonstrate object/number correspondence up to five.

☐ demonstrate the ability to categorize objects into appropriate groupings.

☐ demonstrate the ability to sequence a 3-5 step task.

☐ respond to "wh-" and yes/no questions.

☐ respond to content-related questions pertaining to a literature selection.

☐ follow and/or give one- and two-step oral commands.

☐ demonstrate basic cooking skills by:
    ☐ following a simple recipe.
    ☐ locating appropriate ingredients.
    ☐ locating kitchen tools.

☐ increase pragmatic communication skills by expressing:
    ☐ negation/rejection.
    ☐ requests, wants, and needs.
    ☐ approval.
    ☐ choice selection.
    ☐ reoccurrence (more).
    ☐ greetings.

    verbally or using an appropriate augmented communication system.

☐ read and express 3-5 word sentences using PCS.

Holiday - Related Literature

A Dark, Dark Tale	Ruth Brown
The Magic Pumpkin	Bill Martin, Jr.
One Dark Night	Edna Mitchell Preston
Apples and Pumpkins	Anne Rockwell
Where the Wild Things Are	Maurice Sendak
Pumpkin, Pumpkin	Jeanne Titherington
The Little Old Lady Who Was Not Afraid of Anything	Linda Williams
Halloween Parade	Harriet Ziefert
A Visit to Grandma's	Nancy Carlson
1,2, 3 Thanksgiving!	W. Nikola-Lisa
The Best Train Set Ever	Pat Hutchins
On Christmas Eve	Margaret Wise Brown
Spot's First Christmas	Eric Hill
Five Little Ducks	Raffi

Holiday - Music Resources

"Witches Brew"
"Pack Up the Sleigh"

Witches Brew
Hap Palmer 1976
Educational Activities Inc.
Box 392
Freeport, NY 11520

"Five Little Pumpkins"
"Must Be Santa"

Singable Songs for the Very Young
Raffi 1976
Troubadour Records
Universal City, CA

"Frosty the Snowman"
"We Wish You a Merry Christmas"
"Jingle Bells"

Raffi's Christmas Album
Raffi

"Santa's Coming"
"Thanksgiving Song"

Holiday Songs
Sing & Learn 1987
Macmillan Book Clubs Inc.
Macmillan Educational Co.

Halloween Fun
Lois Skiera-Zucek
Kimbo Educational 1989
P.O. Box 477
Long Branch, NJ 07740

Holiday Songs and Rhythms
Hap Palmer
Eucational Activities, Inc.
Box 392 Freeport, NY 11520

The Twelve Days of Christmas
Tom Glazer
CMS Records, Inc.
226 Washington St.
Mt. Vernon, NY 10553

Holiday - Computer Resources

Bailey's Book House - Edmark   Holiday greeting cards
MAC, IBM

Print Shop Deluxe - Broderbund   Holiday greeting cards
MAC, IBM

Vocabulary Skillbuilder - Edmark   People, family, and holidays
IIe

Everyday is a Holiday - UCLA/LAUSD

Big Pumpkin

by
Erica Silverman

Summary

An old witch plants a pumpkin to make her Halloween party pumpkin pie. The soil must be fertile because this pumpkin grows and grows into a BIG pumpkin, impossible to move. She enlists the aid of a ghost, a vampire, and a mummy, but the pumpkin will not budge. Finally, with an idea from a clever bat, the pumpkin is bounced and rolled into her kitchen. The pie gets made, and the party is saved.

The monsters in this beautifully illustrated book are too funny to be really scary, and children love them. The story features several repeated lines and is fun to act out. This is a wonderful Halloween story.

Suggested Activities

Sharing the Story

Read the story using one of the communication overlays on pages 34-37. This story lends itself well to acting out, so having a big (and heavy) pumpkin available adds to the fun. Let the children take turns pushing and pulling the pumpkin at the appropriate points in the story. (If your pumpkin isn't heavy enough, try holding it still while you pretend to help move it.) Other useful props are pictures or toys representing the other characters in the story, and a small pumpkin for contrast. Martha Stewart types may want to provide some pumpkin pie!

Witch's Brew

Hap Palmer's song, "Witch's Brew," makes a wonderful accompaniment to this activity. Witch's Brew can be made in either a crockpot or in a kettle on the stove. Begin by adding a large bottle of apple cider. As the cider warms, add a variety of ingredients to the pot. Cinnamon sticks are good (let everyone have a good sniff first!), as well as orange or lemon slices. Try adding some cranberry juice if you'd like the color to be a little more interesting. Stir the cauldron with a large spoon, and no good witch cooks without her black hat. Sing the song again as you serve up the brew.
Variation: Have a few extra ingredients available. Nonfood items (the sillier the better) can be presented as potential ingredients for the brew. What goes in a brew? and what doesn't?

Pumpkin Cookies or Ghost Toast

Both of these recipes involve making (and eating) scary faces.

Pumpkin Cookies: Provide each child with a large, store-bought sugar cookie. Give each child a small paper cup filled with a heaping spoonful of vanilla cake frosting. Add one drop each of yellow and red food coloring to every cup. The children then stir with a popsicle stick until the mixture is orange (adjust color if necessary). Assist the children in spreading an orange topping on their cookies. Now for the jack-o-lantern faces. . . add eyes, noses, and mouths of raisins or candy bits—scare your neighbor, then eat!

Ghost Toast: Ghost Toast uses toast instead of cookies, with a topping made by spreading on whipped cream cheese.

Pumpkin Patch Game

All the children sit in a group on the floor holding their pumpkins. Teach the following rhyme and accompanying movements:

> Pumpkin, pumpkin, big and round (Mime a big stomach.)
> Pumpkin, pumpkin, on the ground (Pat the floor.)
> Pumpkin, pumpkin, I'll pick one (Student pats a friend's head.)
> Come with me and have some fun. (Takes friend by the hand; leads to the "pumpkin patch" on the floor.)

One student is chosen to start. As the group says the rhyme, he or she picks a "pumpkin" off the floor and leads him or her to a new spot in the "pumpkin patch" where they sit on the floor. When the verse is said again, the child who was last picked gets to choose the next pumpkin to lead to the patch. Play continues until the pumpkin patch is full of little pumpkins.

HINT: Program this rhyme on an AAC device if you have a nonverbal student in your class.

What Do You Want for Halloween?

Duplicate pages 38-39 for each child. Color the pictures if desired, then cut out the food items on page 39. Using gluesticks, paste the pictures to the trick-or-treat bag as you read the symbol sentences together.

Variation: Use pictures of real food items. The Sunday paper circulars for the week before Halloween are usually full of advertisements for trick-or-treat goodies.

What do I See on Halloween? Make and Take Books

For each child, duplicate one cover page (page 40), and five of the inside pages (page 41). Color these with an orange crayon. Next assist the children in cutting out the pumpkin shaped book pages. Duplicate the picture page (page 42) for each child, and cut the pictures out. Paste these onto the storybook pages as you read the sentences together. Bind along the left edge with staples to create a make-and-take book for reading at school or home.

Trick or Treat Bags

Easy trick-or-treat bags can be made from brown paper lunch sacks. Simple stamp art can be added in various seasonal shapes: pumpkins (orange), bats or witches' hats (black), or ghosts (white). Stamps are a highly accessible way to add decorations and can be made in a variety of ways: potato printing, stamps cut from sponge (craft stores sell flat sponges which are easier to cut, then expand when wet), or fun-foam stamps. Fun foam is sold at craft stores and is thin enough to be cut into shapes with a standard school letter/shape cutter. Mount the cut fun-foam shape onto a block, dip in tempera paint, and stamp away.

Who's in the Ghost House?

Duplicate pages 43 and 44 for each child; color if desired. Cut along the dotted lines to create peek-a-boo windows on the haunted house. Use a gluestick around the edge of the page with just the window shapes on it (page 44), and mount it behind the house page so that the Halloween characters are visible when the windows are opened.

Now read the symbol sentences together as you open each window. The completed peek-a-boo pictures can be mounted on construction paper if desired.

Halloween Concentration

Duplicate the concentration card, page 45, twice to make two card sets. Color the pictures if desired, and cut out the cards. (They will be more durable if mounted onto construction paper squares and laminated.) Play proceeds as in any matching/memory game.

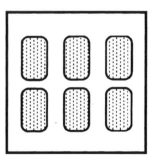

Carryover Activities

Pages 46-48

"Big Pumpkin!"

Communication Overlay B - Wolf

"Big Pumpkin!"	witch	pumpkin pie
ghost	vampire	mummy
bat	pulled and pulled!	"It's big and it's mine!"

Communication Overlay C - Macaw

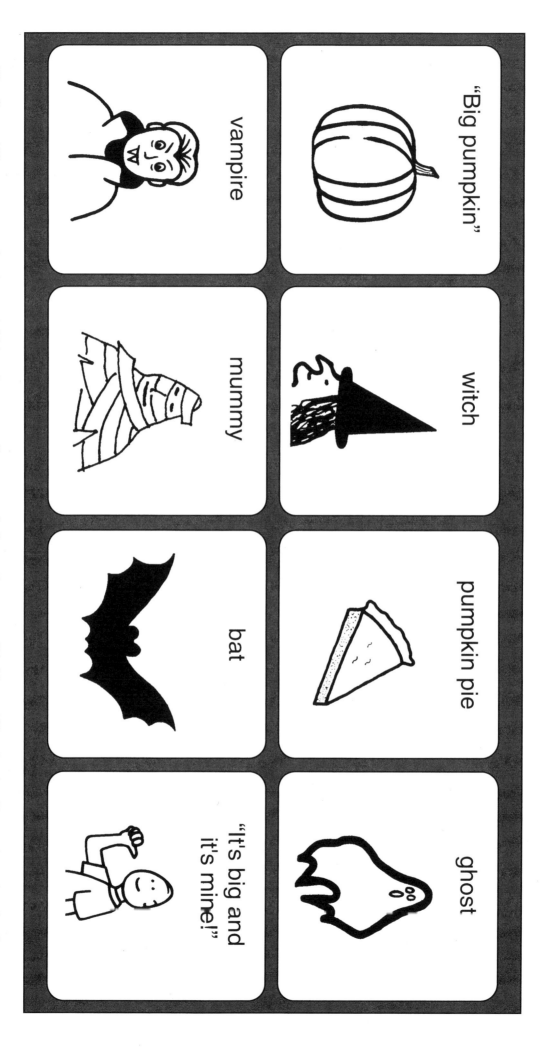

"Big pumpkin"

vampire

witch

mummy

pumpkin pie

bat

ghost

"It's big and it's mine!"

Directions: When programming lower right-hand corner cell, program in the entire verse, "It's big and it's mine but it's stuck on the vine."

Communication Overlay D- Macaw

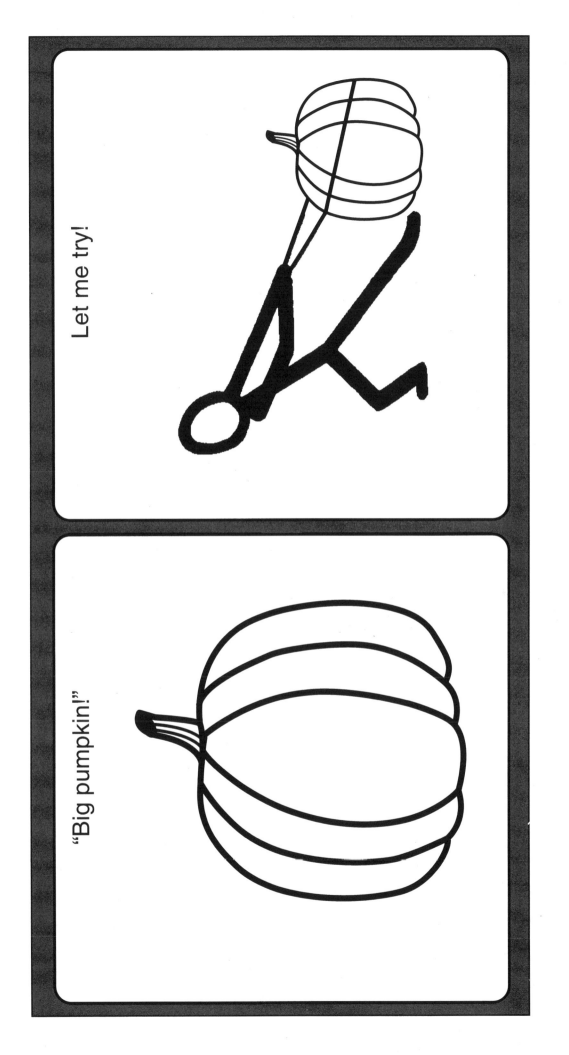

"Big pumpkin!"

Let me try!

What do you want for Halloween?

I want _____ for Halloween .

Big Pumpkin
What do you want for Halloween?

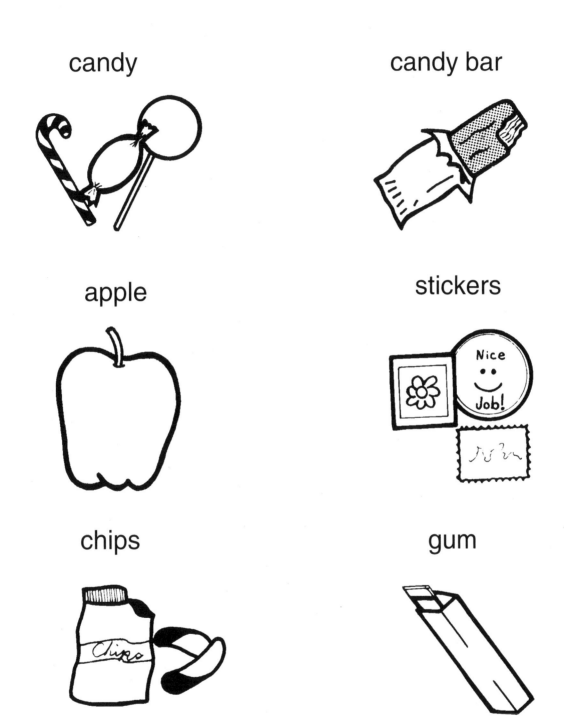

candy

candy bar

apple

stickers

Nice Job!

chips

gum

1. Copy page 38 and 39 for each student.
2. Color if desired, then cut out the food items.
3. Glue each food item onto the trick-or-treat bag as you read the symbol sentences with the student.

What do I see on Halloween?

What do I see on Halloween?

Copy one of this page for each student.

What do I see on Halloween?

I see a ⬜ on Halloween!

Copy five of this page for each student.

What do I see on Halloween?

witch

ghost

bat

pumpkin

black cat

1. For each student, copy the following:
   - (1) - Cover page - found on page 40
   - (5) - Story pages - found on page 41
   - (1) - Picture page - found on page 42
2. Color the storybook pages with an orange crayon, then cut out in the pumpkin shape.
3. Assist students in cutting out the five Halloween pictures on this page.
4. Glue these pictures on the storybook pages as you read the sentences together.
5. Bind with staples along the left edge.

Who's in the Ghost House?

| I | see | _____ | in | house |

43

1. On page 43, cut along dotted lines so doors and windows on haunted house will open.
2. Attach this page to the back of page 43. Glue around the outer edge.
3. As you open the door or window of the haunted house, read the symbol sentence with the student.

Big Pumpkin
Concentration Cards

witch

ghost

bat

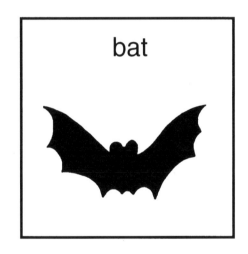

vampire

black cat

jack-o'-lantern

1. Copy this page two times.
2. Cut out the squares to make two identical card sets.
3. If desired, mount on construction paper squares and laminate for durability.

Big Pumpkin
Tell me about it!

1. What did the witch want to cook?

cake	pie	cookies	pizza

- -

2. The witch planted a . . .

flower	bush	pumpkin	tree

- -

3. The pumpkin was too . . .

little	dirty	big
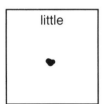		

- -

4. Who helped the witch try to move the pumpkin?

ghost	bat	vampire	dog
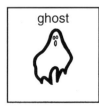	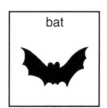		

- -

1. Cut into strips if desired.
2. Children can point to or mark correct answers.

Big Pumpkin
Witch's Rhyme Time

Cut out the bottom row of pictures and paste into the appropriate squares.

1. The  put some pie in his  .

2. The 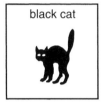 chased a  .

3. The lived in a  .

4. The ate a piece of  .

5. The  lit a nice warm .

- -

  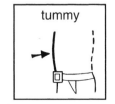  

What's Orange?

cheese

MILK

apple

carrot

orange

pumpkin

1. Identify each food picture.
2. Color the appropriate pictures orange.

Over the River and Through the Wood
by
Lydia Maria Child

Summary

The text of this story is the well—known Thanksgiving song written in 1844 by Lydia Maria Child. (At least we all know the first two lines!) The language is actually somewhat difficult, but is lilting, rhythmic, and features a repeated line. The illustrations by Nadine Bernard Wescott are what gives this book its charm. On every page there is something to look at and talk about. This is a great "stop-and-talk" book.

Suggested Activities

Sharing the Story
Read the story using one of the communication overlays on pages 52-55. The illustrations are excellent. Spend time on each page identifying items and discussing the action. Then try learning the song.

Fun with Music
Although teaching this song may seem difficult, at least the first verse can be easily taught if picture cues are used. Copy and cut out the 8 cue cards on pages 56-57. Teach the song, line by line, or picture by picture. The picture cues can be mounted on a sequence board or held by individual children. You'll be surprised! Add the shake of some bells for a beautiful performance.

Caramel Apples
Another tradition of autumn is making and eating homemade caramel apples. These are easily prepared according to the recipe printed on most caramel candy bags sold in the fall. All that is required is one apple per child, caramels, popsicle sticks, and buttered wax paper for use while the caramel cools on the apples.

Autumn Applesauce

Allow approximately one apple per child to make this recipe. Peel and chop up one or two apples in front of the class (as this is time-consuming, do the remaining apples before class). Place apples in a microwave-safe bowl. Dot the apples with butter, sprinkle with cinnamon, and add lemon juice and sugar to taste if desired. Microwave until soft (time varies with the number of apples). Place the cooked apple mixture into a blender that has been coupled with an environmental-control unit and switch. Blend until pureed. Serve and enjoy. This is better than store-bought!

Duplicate the sequence book pages 58-60 for each child. Cut, color, and assemble books while the apples cook in the microwave. Then enjoy storytime and snacktime together. This is a great opportunity for students to sample textures, smells, and tastes. Try squeezing some lemon juice into a saucer and taste it with and without sugar. Which tastes better? Do you like the smell of cinnamon? Try the soft-cooked apples and the hard crunchy ones. Which is your favorite?

Handprint Turkeys

You will need one piece of heavyweight art paper for each child. On three separate paper plates, place one of the following colors of paint: brown, orange, yellow. Before beginning this activity, have three stamps cut from potato halves or sponges into the following shapes:

beak   wattle   feet

Assist the children in dipping their hands in the brown paint. Keep the **thumb apart** and the **fingers together**. Stamp a handprint onto the art paper. By the time hands have been cleaned, the print is usually dry enough to stamp the remaining three shapes to complete the picture. Draw on an eye with a black marker and your turkey gobbler is ready!

Setting the table for Thanksgiving

Duplicate pages 61-62 for each child. Color the food pictures, then cut out. As you read the symbol sentences together, paste the food pictures on the table. (Gluesticks work best.) What else can you add to the Thanksgiving feast?

I Am Thankful for. . . .
Using the templates on page 63, cut out two circles from brown construction paper. Glue the circles onto a piece of poster board as shown in the illustration. The eyes, beak, and wattle can be drawn with markers or pasted on with colored construction paper.

Using the templates, cut out one feather per child from bright construction paper. Give the children an opportunity to state (or point to!) one thing for which they are thankful. Each child's response is written or drawn on his or her turkey feather. To complete the picture, each child glues his/her feather onto the turkey while expressing his/her own Thanksgiving thought. I am thankful for... my mom, my dad, and chocolate!

Shopping for Thanksgiving Dinner
What would you buy for a Thanksgiving dinner? Turkey or Pizza? Here is your chance to choose!

Collect some of the food advertisement pages from the Sunday paper (a week or two before Thanksgiving there are lots of seasonal and not-so-seasonal food items). Duplicate the shopping cart on page 64 for each child. As the children choose what they would buy, cut out the pictures of these food items and glue them in the shopping cart as you read the symbol sentences together. You are bound to have some interesting Thanksgiving dinners!

Carryover Activities

Pages 65-67

Communication Overlay A - Wolf

Over the river and through the wood. . .

Communication Overlay B - Macaw

It's Thanksgiving Day!

Over the river and through the wood. . .

Communication Overlay C - Wolf

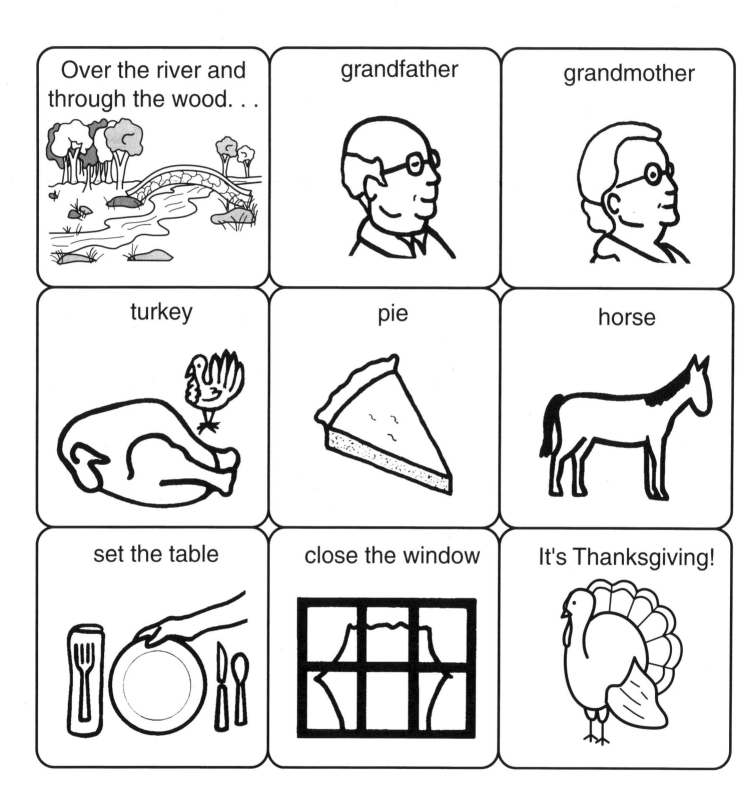

Over the river and through the wood. . .

grandfather

grandmother

turkey

pie

horse

set the table

close the window

It's Thanksgiving!

Communication Overlay D - Macaw

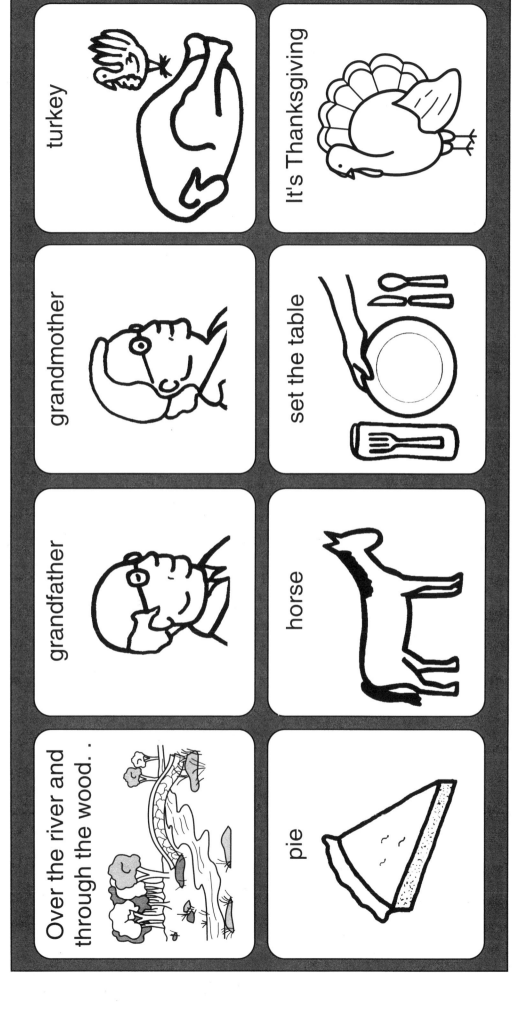

through the white
and drifted snow

oh how the wind does blow!

it stings the toes, and bites the nose

as over the ground we go!

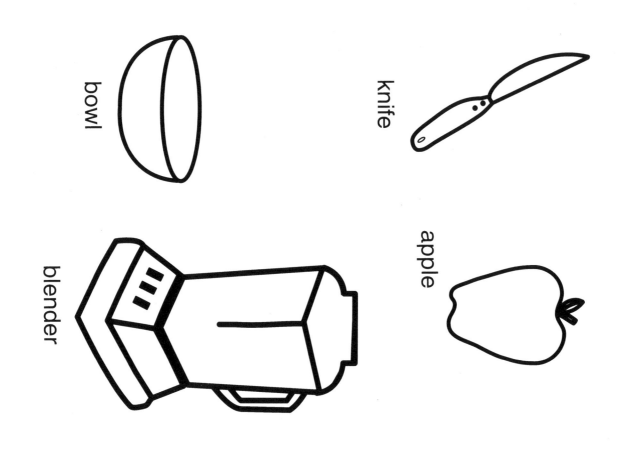

bowl

knife

blender

apple

I   cut   the   apples .

58

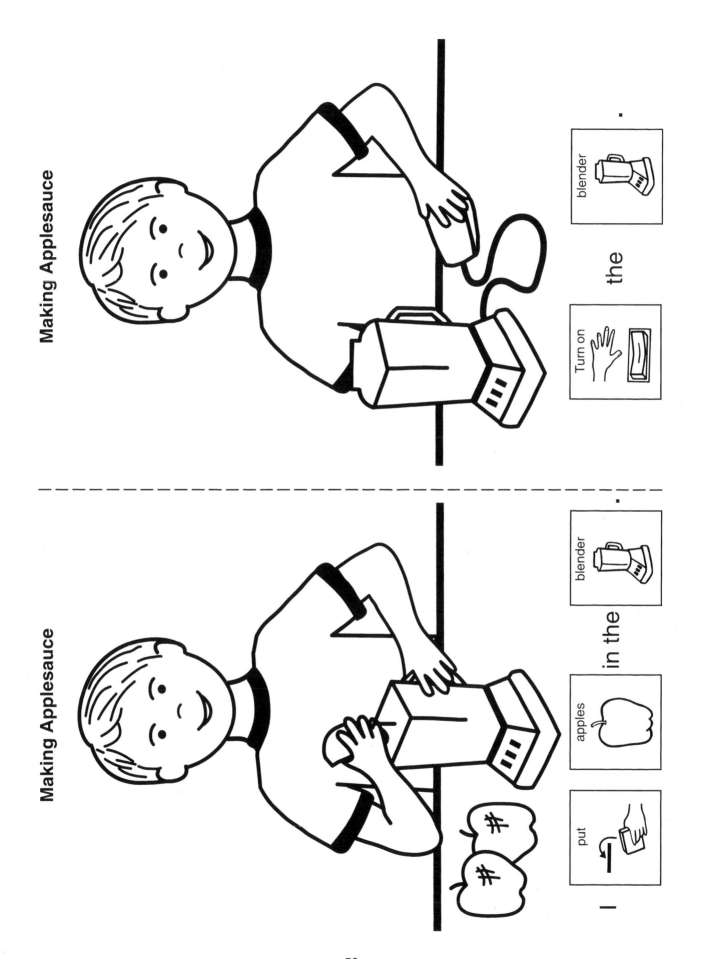

Making Applesauce

Turn on the blender.

Making Applesauce

put apples in the blender.

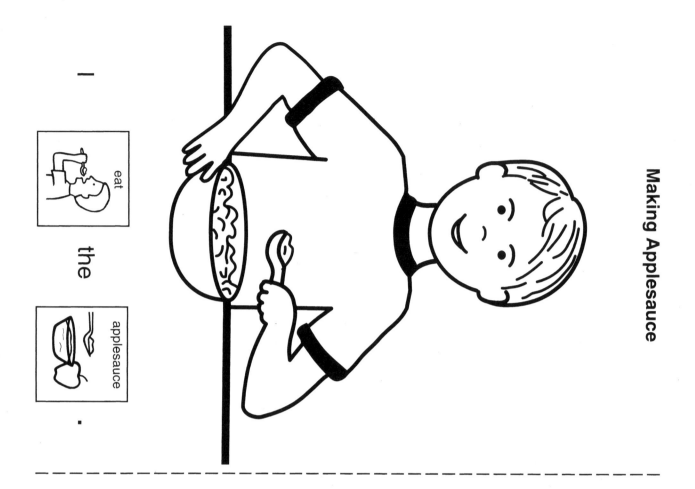

I _____ the _____ .

eat

applesauce

Set the table for Thanksgiving

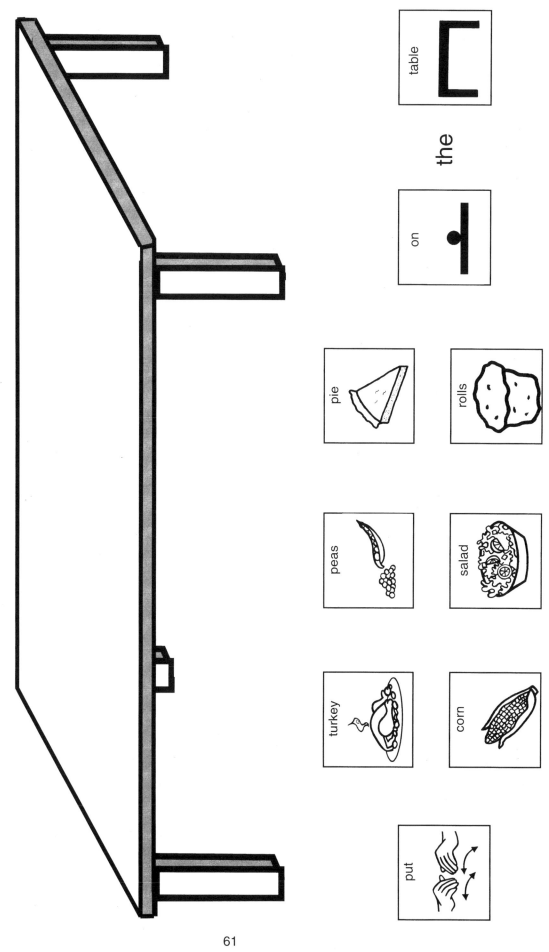

table

the

on

pie

rolls

peas

salad

turkey

corn

put

61

Set the table for Thanksgiving

salad

turkey

corn

rolls

pie

peas

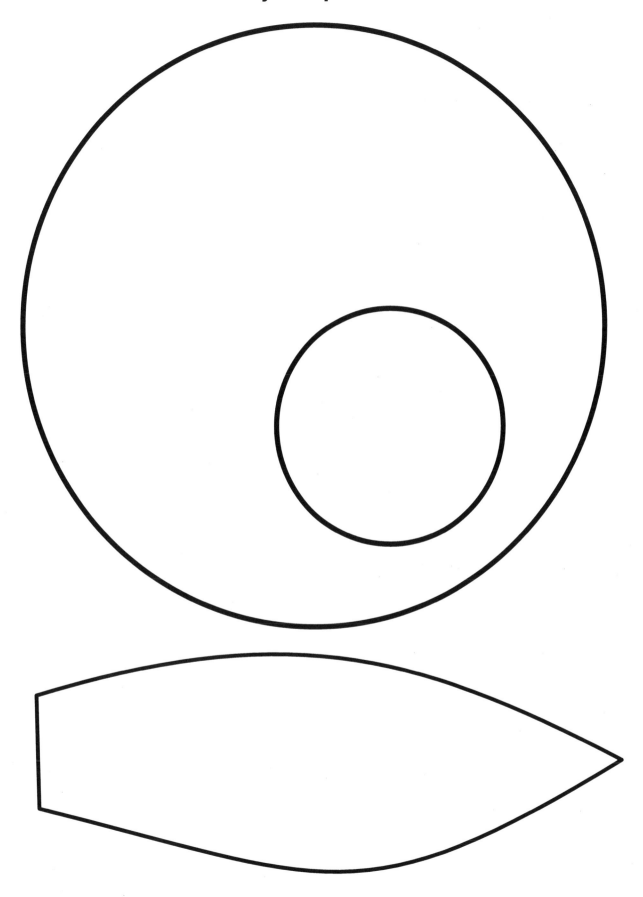

Thanksgiving dinner . . . What should I buy?

I want _____ for Thanksgiving.

Over the River and Through the Wood
Tell Me About It

1. What holiday is in this story?

Christmas	Halloween	Thanksgiving	Valentine's Day

2. The family is going to visit. . .

grandfather	policeman	fireman	grandmother

3. What are they going to eat?

pizza	turkey dinner	pie	french fries

4. The weather was. . .

snowy	rainy	hot

Instructions:
1. Cut into strips if desired.
2. Circle or mark correct answers.

Tell Me About It

1. Find the meats:

turkey	apple	ham	bacon	corn
		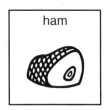	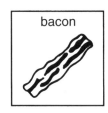	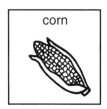

---

2. Find the vegetables:

hamburger	corn	bread	peas	potato
				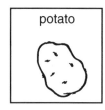

---

3. Find the fruits:

apple	orange	pizza	banana	hot dog
	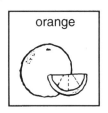			

---

4. Find the desserts:

taco	pie	cookies	spaghetti	cake
	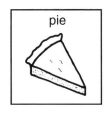			

---

1. Cut into strips, if desired.
2. Circle or mark correct answers.

What do we eat for . . . ?

Draw a line from food item to the meal.

dinner

turkey dinner

pancakes

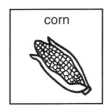

corn

cereal

toast

breakfast

Corduroy's Christmas

by
Don Freeman

Summary

Corduroy, an overstuffed, slightly ragtag teddy bear, is a familiar friend to many children. This beautifully illustrated story follows Corduroy as he prepares for Christmas. He decorates his tree, bakes cookies, wraps presents, writes to Santa, and goes caroling with friends. He hangs his stocking on Christmas Eve, and on Christmas morning awakes to find that Santa has indeed visited during the night. This is a charming book that is full of Christmas time activities. It is a "lift-the-flap" book, which is an ideal way to ensure participation during storytime.

Suggested Activities

Sharing the Story

This is a great story to start with a song. Try teaching "Must Be Santa" (see music activity next section), or use any familiar Christmas song such as "Jingle Bells" or "We Wish You a Merry Christmas." Read the story using overlays on pages 72-73. The full-page illustrations are full of colorful, clear pictures of Christmasy events and items, so on subsequent readings it's fun to stop and talk about each page.

Santa Sing-a-Long

The song "Must Be Santa" (recorded by Raffi) is one that children love to sing. Despite its length, it can easily be taught if visual cues are used. Copy the picture cards on pages 74-78. Color if desired, then cut out. These can be used as visual cues by either mounting on a display board in sequential order, or by gluing to popsicle sticks and holding up each one in the proper order as you sing. Use body movements or sign language and/or props (cherry nose, beard that's white, cap on head, etc.) to add to the fun. This is a perfect song to perform in Christmas programs.

Crunchy Christmas Trees

Give each child an ice cream cone (sugar cone variety). Put a good sized spoonful of canned vanilla cake frosting in a paper cup, one per child. Add a drop of green food coloring, and let the children mix the color into the frosting with a Popsicle stick or spoon until the frosting is green. Spread the frosting on the cone (pointed end up) to create a Christmas tree. Decorate your tree with raisins, chocolate chips, or candy pieces. The trees make a beautiful display, if you can keep from eating them first!

Christmas Cookies
Don't forget to join Corduroy in his Christmas baking. We generally use store-bought, refrigerated sugar cookie dough. You will need a rolling pin and extra flour to keep the dough from sticking to table tops (or children's fingers!) Give each child his or her own portion to roll and cut out into Christmas shapes with cookie cutters. It's easier if the dough has remained chilled until right before using. Offer a choice of red or green sprinkles to decorate, and bake according to package directions. Yum!

Decorate the Christmas Tree
If you plan to have a Christmas tree, making the decorations is a great classroom activity. Make a garland from loops of colored construction paper. Some children will be able to cut the paper strips themselves, and this is a good opportunity to incorporate choice-making for colors.

Make snowflake ornaments to hang on the tree. Glue 4 popsicle sticks together as shown in the picture. When dry, paint each one white and sprinkle with silver glitter. Let dry again, and the snowflakes are ready to decorate the tree.

What's in Santa's Sleigh?
Duplicate the sleigh picture on page 79. Provide several toy catalogs for each table (such as "Toys-R-Us," Sunday paper circulars, etc.). Assist the children in cutting out pictures of the things they want for Christmas, and paste them into Santa's sleigh. Then read the symbol sentences together. This is a picture version of a letter to Santa.

Letters to Santa
Reproduce the letter to Santa (page 80) for each child. Let each child choose a toy he or she wants, and draw in its picture on the letter. The children should sign their letters in the appropriate place. These can be used for display, or passed along to Santa!
Variation: Children can cut and paste a toy picture from a magazine or catalog.

What Goes on the Christmas Tree?

Duplicate the Christmas tree activity (pages 81 and 82) for each child. Color the Christmas tree; also identify and color each decoration before cutting out. Now decorate the Christmas tree, pasting on the ornaments as you read the accompanying symbol sentences.

Peek-a-Boo Presents

Duplicate the Peek-a-Boo presents activity for each child (pages 83 and 84). The toy pictures can be colored if desired. Cut along the dotted lines to create peek-a-boo flaps. Line up the two pages and staple or glue to construction paper to mount. This makes a readable picture to share at home or school.

Playtime Overlays — Corduroy's Christmas Day

Duplicate the overlays for Wolf or Macaw (pages 85 or 86) and color. Program in messages according to the charts provided on page 89, and mount on the communication device. Now you have a "talking overlay" for independent or group play.

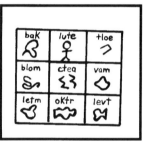

Carryover Activities

Pages 87-88

Communication Overlay A - Wolf

Corduroy 	Christmas tree 	baking cookies 
wrap the presents 	letter to Santa 	sing Christmas carols 
It's Santa! 	Look! Look! 	My turn! 

Communication Overlay B - Macaw

| Corduroy | Christmas tree | baking cookies | wrap the presents |
| letter to Santa | sing Christmas carols | It's Santa! | My turn! |

Must be Santa

beard that's long and white

special night

Must be Santa

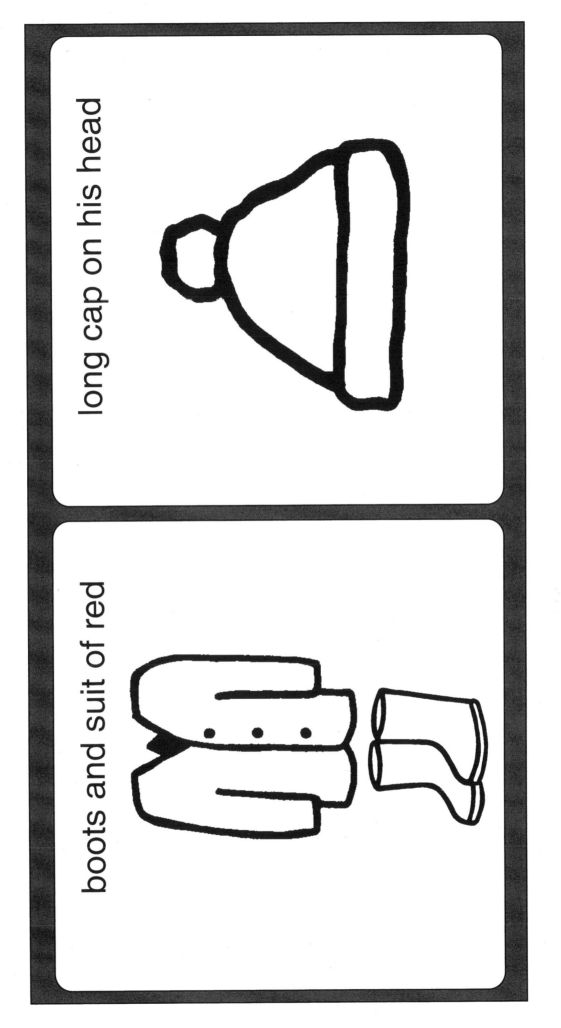

long cap on his head

boots and suit of red

cherry nose

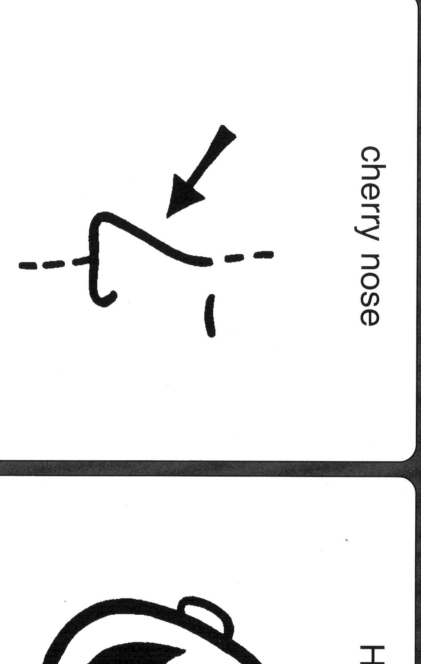

Ho, ho, ho!

Must be Santa

8 little reindeer

Come our way!

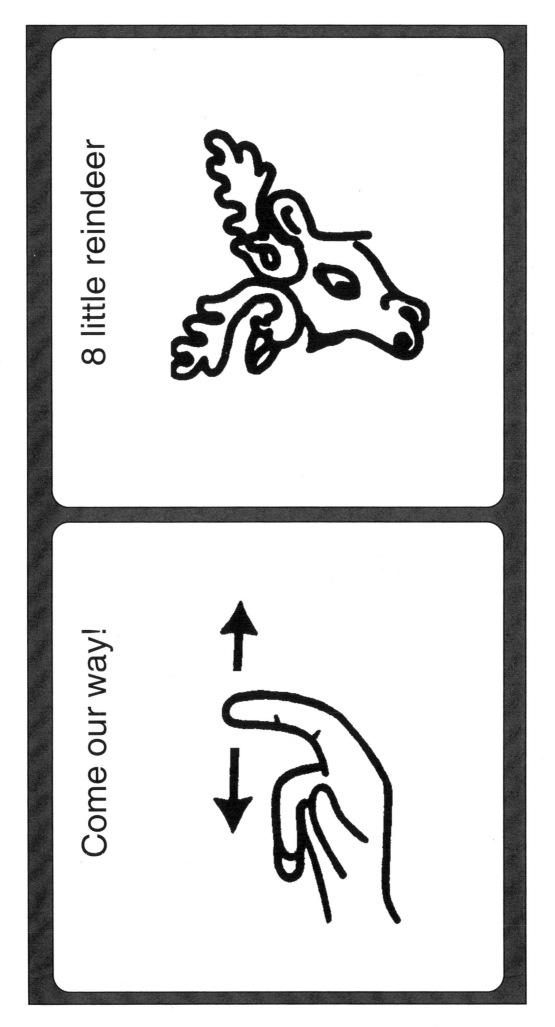

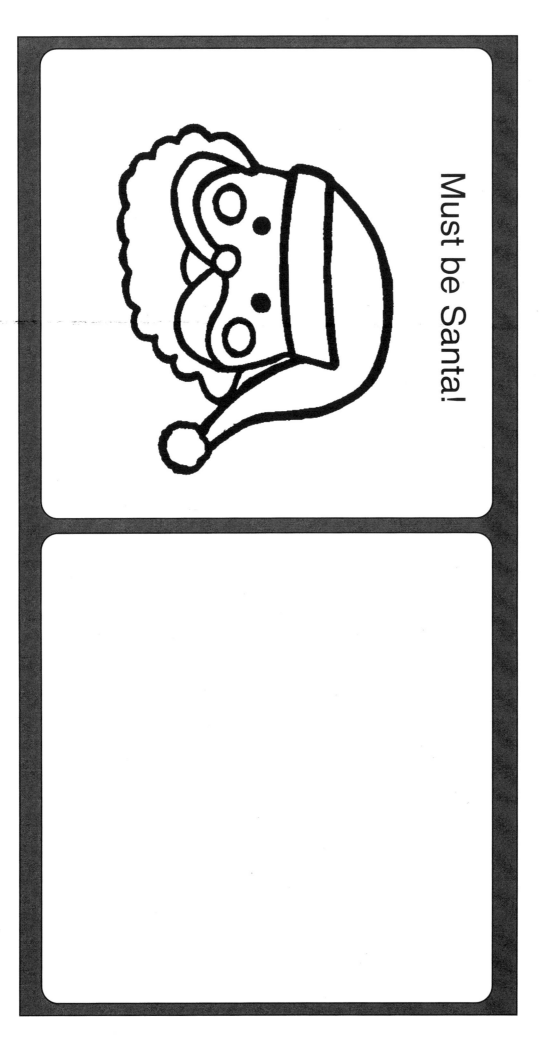

Must be Santa!

Must be Santa

What's in Santa's Sleigh?

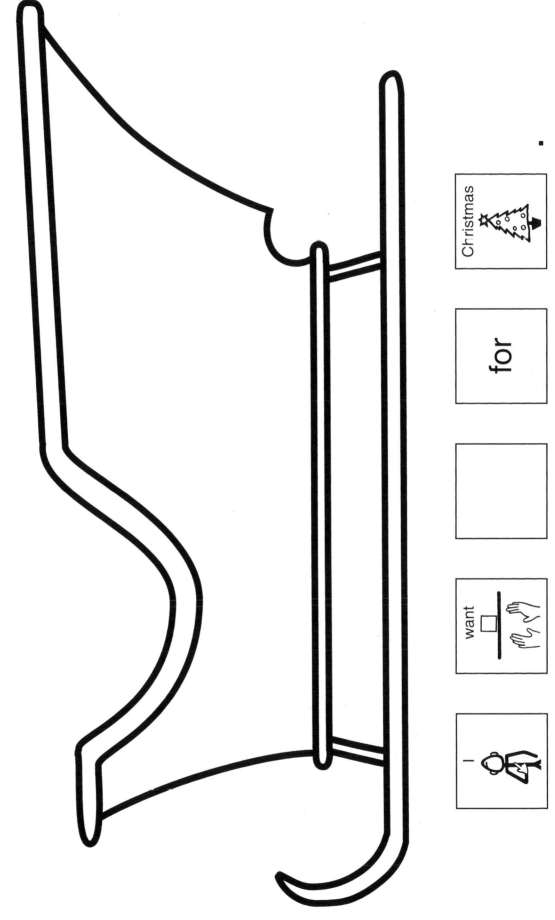

Letter to Santa

Dear Santa,

Please send me a

Love,

_____
(name)

Decorate the Tree

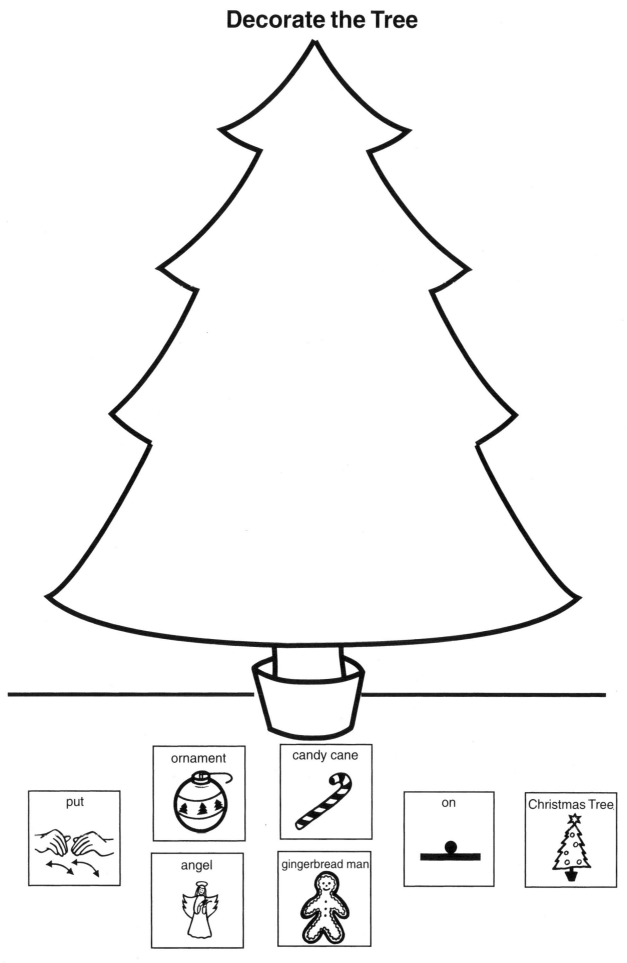

put

ornament

candy cane

angel

gingerbread man

on

Christmas Tree

Decorate the Christmas Tree

Cut on dotted lines, then attach ornaments to tree on previous page.

Peek-a-Boo Presents

| Corduroy | got | | for | Christmas |

Cut on dotted lines, then place page on top of presents on next page.

Peek-a-Boo Presents

ball

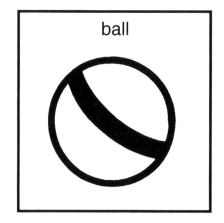

sweater

train

puzzle

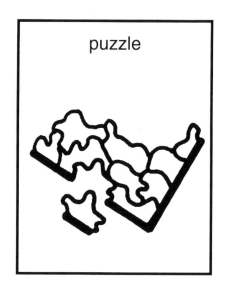

truck

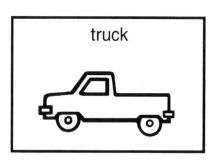

WOLF Playtime Overlay

MACAW Playtime Overlay

Tell Me About It
Which object is different?

Directions: Circle the different object in each row.

1.

 cookie

 cake

 cookie

 cookie

2.

 present

 present

 present

 letter

3.

 bear

 bear

 dog

 bear

4.

 tape

 scissors

 scissors

 scissors

Tell Me About It

1. Corduroy is a

---

2. What did Corduroy make for his friends?

---

3. Corduroy wrote a letter to

 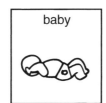  

---

4. What presents did Corduroy find under his tree?

 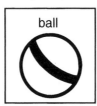  

---

5. What did Corduroy need to wrap presents?

 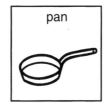  

1. Cut into strips if desired.
2. Children can point to or mark correct answers.

88

Wolf and Macaw Playtime Overlays
Programming Instructions

Wolf overlay, 9 location

1	2	3
4	5	6
7	8	9

1 and 4	What's under the Christmas tree?
2 and 3	It's Santa Claus!
5	I see some presents.
6	Merry Christmas, Corduroy!
7 and 8	It's a train!
9	Corduroy got a ball!

Macaw overlay, 8 location

1	2	3	4
5	6	7	8

1 and 5	What's under the Christmas tree?
2	Merry Christmas, Corduroy!
3 and 4	It's Santa Claus!
6	I see some presents!
7 and 8	Corduroy got a train!

The Gingerbread Man

Traditional

Summary

"Run, run, as fast as you can, you can't catch me, I'm the gingerbread man!" Though not strictly a holiday story, we have always shared this story during the winter holiday season. Something about the smell of gingerbread, perhaps?

There are many beautiful versions of this old folk tale available. We have chosen the edition published by Scholastic, due to its wide availability in school libraries, and ease of ordering. Also, a few other versions use vocabulary that is unfamiliar to most modern children, such as threshers, reapers, and mowers. However, if you find a version you like better, minor changes to the overlays provided should render them suitable.

Suggested Activities

Sharing the Story

This is definitely a story that becomes more and more fun each time it is read. So be sure to share it several times, especially before each related activity. As children learn the repeated line "run, run..." or know where to access it on their communication device, they love to chime in.

Use one of the communication overlays provided on pages 94-97 when reading. Toy props representing the people and animals in the story are easy to assemble and many variety/discount stores sell a relatively cheap gingerbread man toy during the holiday season. Children love acting out the chase in this tale, so props or pictures are a must!

Gingerbread Men

After reading the story, you'll want to make your own gingerbread men. This is a wonderful opportunity to focus on body parts-- especially faces. Use the recipe that comes with gingerbread cake mix, and add raisins and candy pieces for decoration.

After the dough is mixed and rolled out, use a cookie cutter to press out the gingerbread men (or ladies). Bake according to package directions. After baking, press in the eyes, nose, etc., with the raisins or candy. Do this while the cookies are still warm. If desired, use colored frosting to add clothing (squeeze bottles sold for cake decorations work well). Now eat them quickly before they run away! Communication overlays for this activity are found on pages 98-99.

Cinnamon-Applesauce Ornaments

Mix 1/2 cup applesauce and 2/3 cup ground cinnamon in a bowl. Stir until well mixed. Knead to form a ball of stiff dough. (If you let the children knead, be sure and wash hands afterwards and avoid contact with eyes.) Dust the table with more cinnamon and roll the dough with a rolling pin to a thickness of about 1/4 inch. Using cookie cutters dusted with cinnamon, cut out a variety of holiday shapes. Use a straw to cut a small hole near the top for hanging. Lift the shapes with a pancake turner. Place on a tray that is lined with wax paper for drying. The ornaments will need to dry thoroughly (2-3 days) and can then be decorated.

This recipe will make 4-6 ornaments depending on the shapes. It can be doubled or tripled to fit the size or your class. When they are dry, squeeze on designs or decorations with a glue bottle, then dust with glitter. Add a bow or red yarn to the top to make a hanger. These ornaments are long lasting and have a delightful smell. They make wonderful holiday gifts or tree decorations.

Gingerbread Faces

Provide each of the children with a white paper plate. Help them color these with brown crayons. Have available precut shapes made from construction paper—2 triangles for the eyes, a circle for the nose, and crescent shapes for the mouth. Assist the children in selecting, identifying, and gluing on each body part. If desired, have a pile of precut strands of yarn. Glue the yarn above the face to add a topping of hair. These make a cheerful bulletin board, or they can be hung as mobiles throughout the room.

What's in the Oven?

Duplicate pages 100-101 for each child. Color the pictures on each page if desired, then cut out the picture wheel. On the stove picture, cut along the dotted lines so that the oven door will fold open. Place the picture wheel behind the first page and fasten where indicated with a two-prong metal fastener. Now when you open the oven door, you should see something tasty cooking. As you move the picture wheel to change the contents of the oven, practice reading the symbol sentences together. You can make this beginning literacy activity even more fun if you add some real-life munchies.

Gingerbread Twins

Duplicate the gingerbread figures on pages 102-103 two times. Cut out the two sets of gingerbread men. (If you'd like to keep this game for future use, the figures are more durable if glued onto construction paper backing and laminated.) Play proceeds as in any concentration or memory game. The figures are placed face down on the table. Each child in turn chooses two figures and keeps them if they match. If they don't match, they are returned to the table. Play ends when all the gingerbread pairs have been found. Besides being fun, this is a great game for practicing visual matching and same and different concepts.

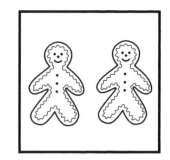

Carryover Activities

Pages 104-107

Run, run, as fast as you can!
You can't catch me,
I'm the gingerbread man!

Communication Overlay B - Macaw

gingerbread man

Run, run, as fast as you can!

Programming note: Program entire message in the lower right cell: Run, run, as fast as you can, you can't catch me, I'm the gingerbread man!"

Communication Overlay C - Wolf

Programming note: Program entire message in the lower right cell: Run, run, as fast as you can, you can't catch me, I'm the gingerbread man!"

Communication Overlay D - Macaw

gingerbread man	old woman	little boy	farmer
bear	wolf	fox	Run, run!

Programming note: Program entire message in the lower right cell: Run, run, as fast as you can, you can't catch me, I'm the gingerbread man!"

Communication Overlay E - Wolf

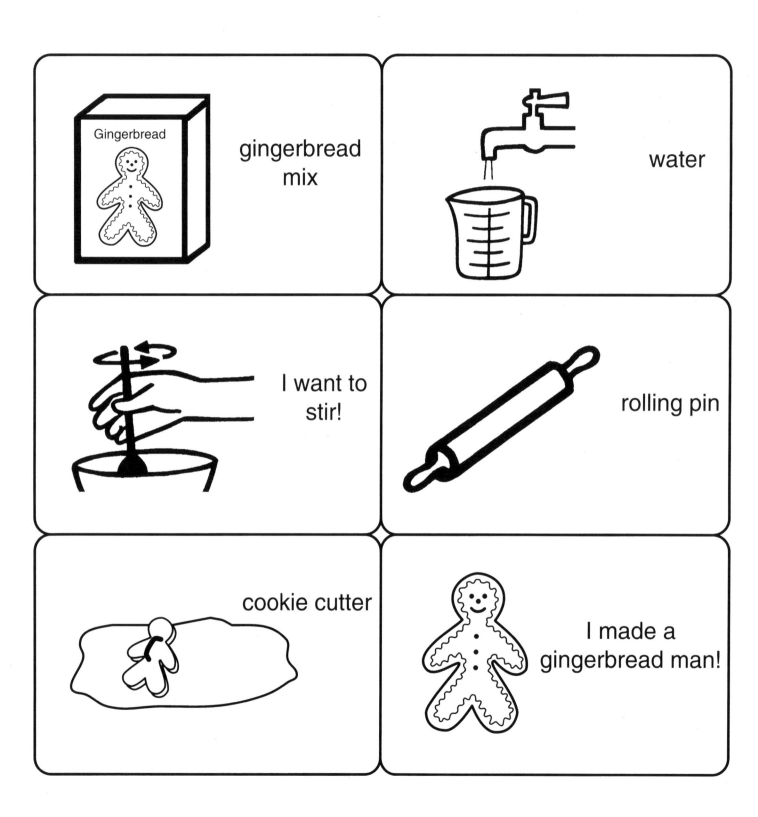

gingerbread mix

water

I want to stir!

rolling pin

cookie cutter

I made a gingerbread man!

Communication Overlay F - Macaw

| rolling pin | I want to stir | Put in some water. | gingerbread mix |
| I made a gingerbread man! | Put them in the oven. | Put them on a cookie sheet. | cookie cutter |

Gingerbread

The Gingerbread Man
What's in the oven?

Cut along dotted lines

The    .

The Gingerbread Man
Picture Wheel

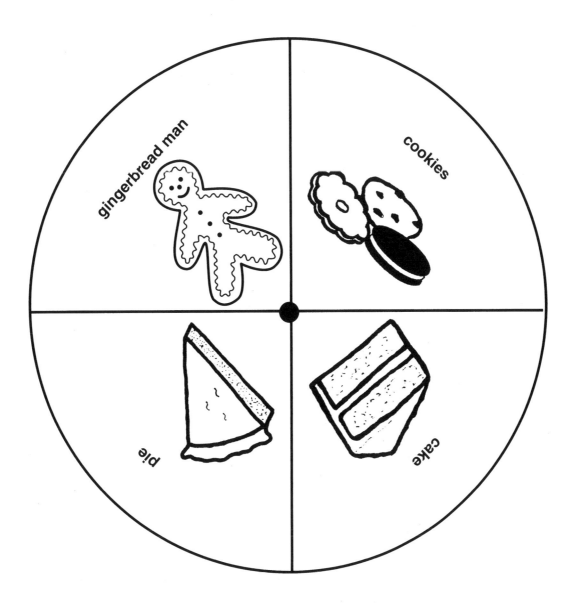

1. Color worksheet pages if desired.

2. Cut out oven door opening where indicated. Cut out picture wheel.

3. Using a two-prong metal fastener, fasten the picture wheel behind the oven so that the pictures can be viewed when the oven door is open.

4. Turn the wheel as you read the symbol sentences.

Gingerbread Twins - 1

1. Duplicate this page and the following page two times.
2. Cut out the gingerbread figures.
3. Play proceeds as in a concentration/memory game.

The Gingerbread Man
Tell Me About It

Circle the appropriate symbol, and read the sentences together.

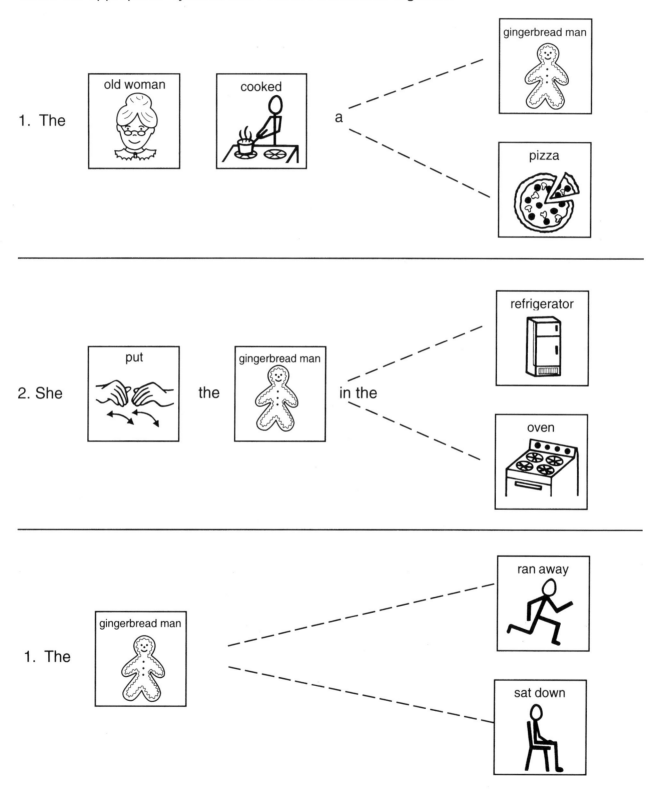

1. The [old woman] [cooked] a [gingerbread man] / [pizza]

2. She [put] the [gingerbread man] in the [refrigerator] / [oven]

1. The [gingerbread man] [ran away] / [sat down]

The Gingerbread Man
Ready to cook...but what do we need?
Name and color the kitchen tools

rolling pin

measuring spoons

pan

hammer

mixer

scissors

measuring cup

The Gingerbread Man

Put away our cooking things...where do they go?

Draw a line from each food item to where it goes in the kitchen.

refrigerator

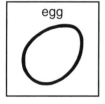
egg

cake mix

milk

sugar

butter

cupboard

The Gingerbread Man
Tell Me About It

1. What did the old lady cook?

- -

2. What did the gingerbread man do?

- -

3. Who tried to catch the gingerbread man?

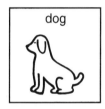

- -

4. Who ate the gingerbread man?

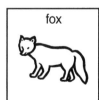

- -

1. Cut into strips if desired.
2. Children can point to or mark correct answers.

Easter Parade
by
Mary Chalmers

Summary

Every spring, chickens, rabbits, and ducks all gather at the Easter farm. There they make Easter baskets for all the forest animals and load their wagon for the Easter Parade. They distribute their baskets to all the forest children, but one little basket remains. Who didn't get a basket? They finally find the sleeping ladybug and leave her basket by her tiny bed. This story is filled with wonderful illustrations. On every page there is something to look at and talk about.

Suggested Activities

Sharing the Story

Read this story around a table if you are planning to go straight to the Easter basket or dyeing Easter eggs activity. Communication overlays are provided on pages 112 and 113. Suggested story props are toys or pictures of chickens, rabbits, and ducks, an Easter basket, and several plastic eggs. If the eggs are distributed among several children, they can follow the story by putting them in the Easter basket together. What can go in an Easter basket besides eggs?

Where's the Egg? Make-and-Take Book

Duplicate the make-and-take books, pages 114-118 for each child. The pictures can be colored if desired. Cut out the squares on the first 4 pages to create peek-a-boo windows framing the egg on the last page. (It's especially fun if the egg has been colored as a brightly decorated Easter egg.) Bind the book with construction paper and staple. It's ready to read and share!

Dyeing Eggs Sequence

Duplicate pages 119 and 120 for each child. Cut out each page of the sequence book and color with crayons. The child reads the symbol sentences as the pages are placed in correct order. Bind with staples to create a book to read out loud and share at home.

Dyeing Easter Eggs

Hard boil and chill at least one egg per child prior to beginning this activity. Obtain an Easter Egg dye kit from the store. Use clear plastic cups to mix the colors so the children can see the transformation as the eggs are dunked. Use the communication overlays on pages 121 or 122 to help in the selection of colors.

Another fun activity is using a crayon-resist technique. Children decorate their eggs with their names or a design using a crayon. The designs show up beautifully when the eggs are dyed. Now all you need are Easter baskets to be ready for an egg hunt!

Easter Egg Baskets

An easy basket can be made by cutting the top off brown paper lunch bags. The bag should stand about 6 inches in height. Fold the bag flat for decorating. The bags can be decorated with any combination of crayons, paints, or glitter. Another method is potato-printing or sponge-printing egg shapes in different colors onto the bag. Cut 2 potatoes in half and carve out an egg shape on each half. Or, cut egg shapes from dry kitchen sponges. Provide paper plates with 4 different colors of paint. The children select the colors and stamp away. After decorating, staple on a handle made of poster board strips cut to size.

Playtime Overlays--Easter Egg Hunt

Duplicate the playtime overlays for Wolf or Macaw on pages 123 to 126. Please note that these overlays consist of two sheets each. On the top sheet, cut along the dotted lines where indicated to create "lift-the-flap" openings. Color the top sheet if desired. On the bottom sheet, color the eggs a different color for each egg. Place the sheets on top of each other lined up so that when a student lifts the flap he or she will find an egg. Glue around the edges to hold the two layers together. Mount onto your communication device, and program messages to correspond to the lift-the-flap openings. Suggested messages are given on page127. This creates a "talking" lift-the-flap picture that can be used for independent play or during teaching activities.

Musical Egg Hunt

Try singing this song right after reading the story. To the melody of the traditional folk song "Muffin Man," sing:

> Have you seen the Easter egg,
> the Easter egg, The Easter egg,
> Have you seen the Easter egg,
> The egg is (in/on/under. . .).

For each verse, place a plastic egg somewhere different—under the chair, on the table, etc. Sing the location in the song's last line. For more fun, let a child hide the egg while the others close their eyes. This song also goes well as part of a regular Easter egg hunt.

Carryover Activities

Pages 128-131

Communication Overlay A - Wolf

chickens	rabbits	ducks
Easter basket	Easter eggs	animal children
Who didn't get a basket?	The ladybug!	Turn the page.

Communication Overlay B - Macaw

Make-and-Take Book

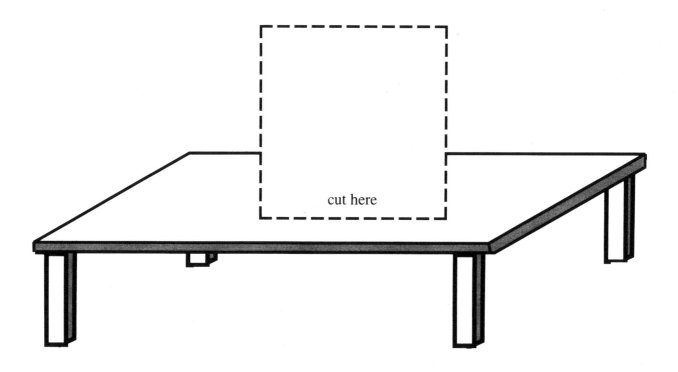

cut here

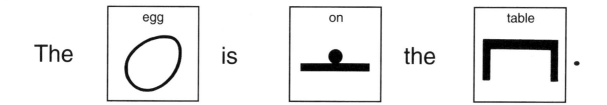

The egg is on the table.

Where's the Egg?
Make-and-Take Book

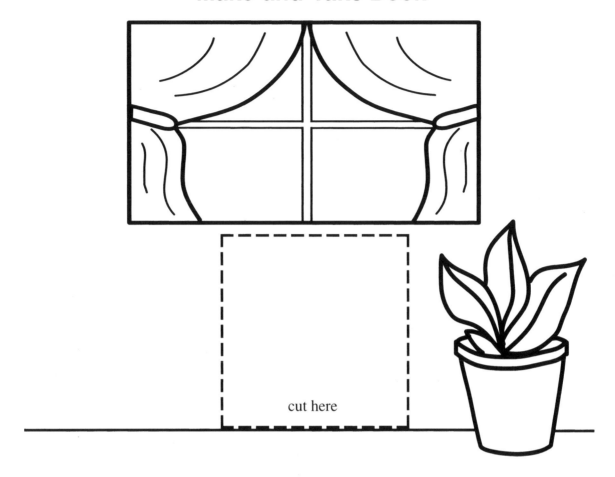

cut here

The 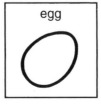 is 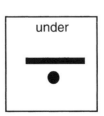 the 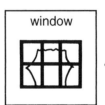 .

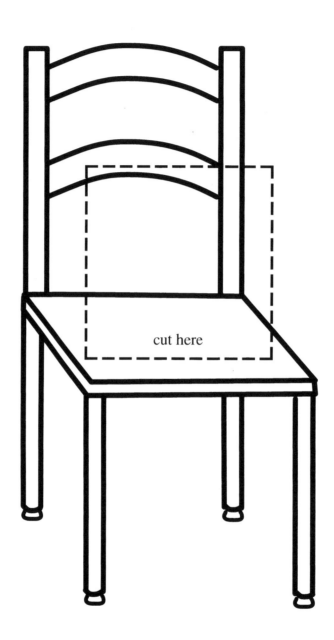

The 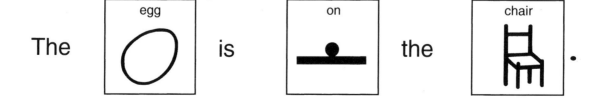 is the .

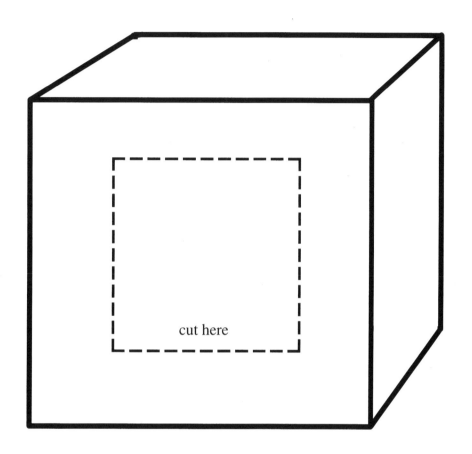

cut here

The 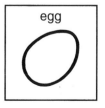 is  the 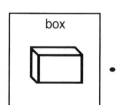 .

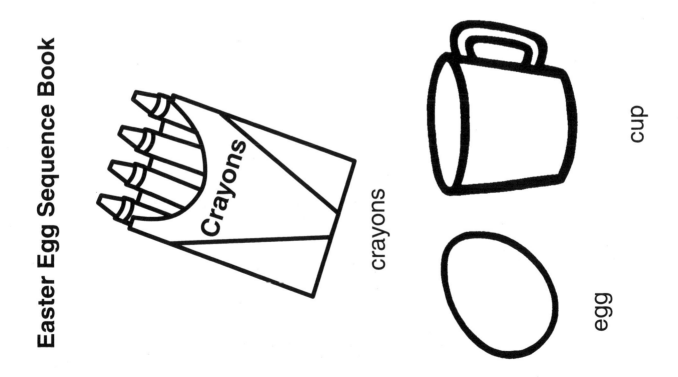

1 draw | on the | egg .

Easter Egg Sequence Book

crayons

cup

egg

119

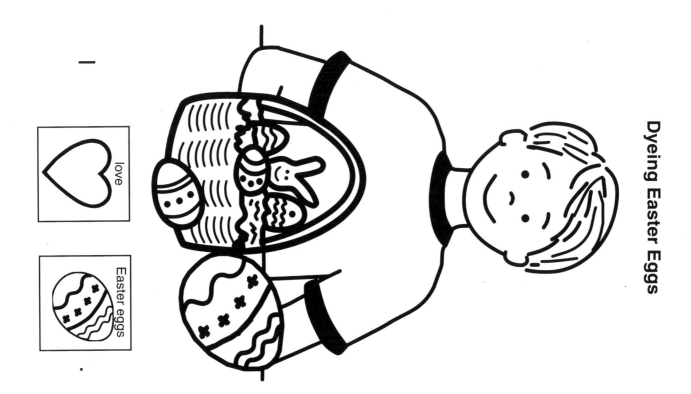

_ dye the egg .

_ love Easter eggs .

Communication Overlay C - Wolf

egg

red

green

cup

yellow

blue

crayon

Let's dip the egg.

my turn

Instructions:
Color in the color symbol circles.

Communication Overlay D - Macaw

Instructions:
Color in the color symbol circles.

egg

cup

crayon

Let's dip the egg.

red

yellow

green

blue

Playtime Overlay - Wolf

The | egg | is

cut here

cut here

cut here

cut here

Playtime Overlay (pg 2) - Wolf

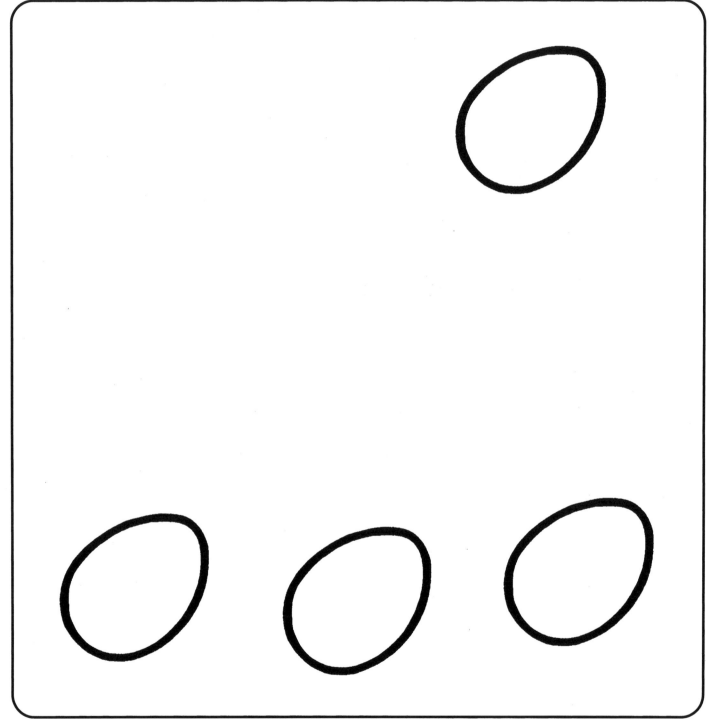

Instructions:
1. Color each egg a different color.
2. Place behind Playtime overlay, page 123.
3. Glue around the edges to attach.
4. Program the WOLF according to instructions on page 127.

Playtime Overlay - Macaw

The [egg   ] is

Playtime Overlay - Macaw

Instructions:
1. Color each egg a different color.
2. Place behind Playtime overlay, page125.

3. Glue around the edges to attach.
4. Program the WOLF according to instructions on page127.

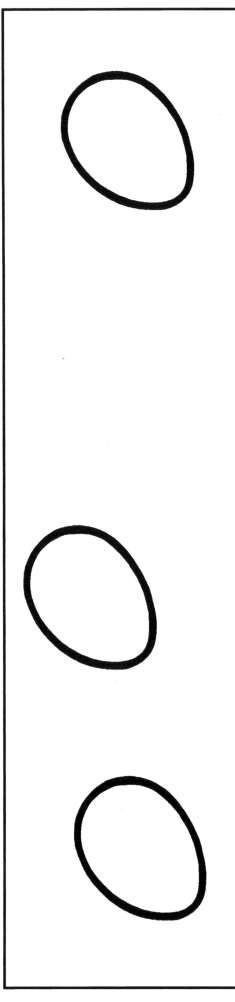

Easter Parade Playtime Overlays
Programming Instructions

Wolf overlay, 9 location

1	2	3
4	5	6
7	8	9

1	The egg is
2 and 3	in the basket
7	under the tree
8	in the bush
9	in the flowers

Macaw overlay, 8 location

1	2	3	4
5	6	7	8

1	The egg is
2	in the basket
5	in the flowers
7	under the slide
8	under the tree

Note: Some teachers may prefer replacing the location messages with color words; e.g., the egg is red, etc.

The Easter Parade
Tell Me About It

1. What animals are in the parade?

chicken

rabbit

lion

duck

---

2. What do they put in the Easter baskets?

hamburger

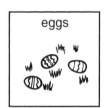
eggs

hot dog

candy

---

3. On the day of the parade it was. . .

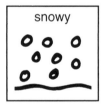
snowy

rainy

sunny

---

4. Who didn't get a basket?

snake

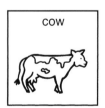
cow

ladybug

horse

Instructions:
1. Cut into strips if desired.
2. Children can point to or mark correct answers.

Which animal is different?
Tell Me About It

1.

chicken	chicken	horse	chicken

2.

fish	duck	duck	duck

3.

rabbit	rabbit	rabbit	snake

4.

mouse	lion	mouse	mouse

Instructions:
Draw a circle around the different animal in each row.

Easter Parade
How Many Eggs!

Instructions:
Match the eggs with the correct number and color.

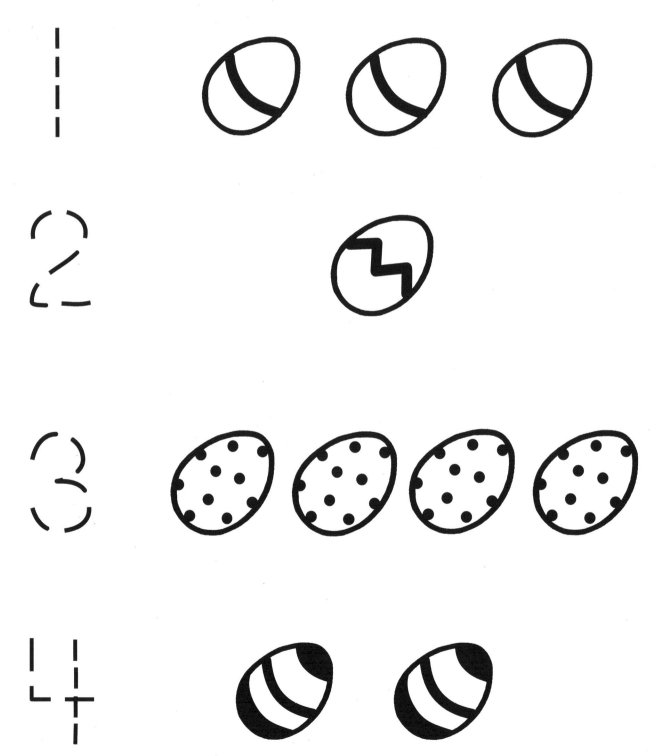

Match the Easter Eggs!

Draw your own!

Family Fun Unit

Family Fun Unit

Introduction

A child's world begins with the family. Communication, social skills, and early learning all find their origin in the family setting. Each child's home experiences are unique and special to him or her. Sharing family differences as well as similarities is a highly motivating topic for children. They naturally enjoy reading about families and sharing their own wealth of knowledge.

The books in this unit are just a few of the many children's literature selections based on the family theme. **Select the stories and suggested activities in this unit that work best for you and certainly add others.**

Literature Selections
See page 360 for book sources.
(Note: This unit can be completed using all or a portion of the books listed below.)

All by Myself. Mercer Mayer (1983). A Golden Book., Western Publishing Co., Racine,
    Wisconsin, 53404.
    ISBN: 0-307-11938-6
    ISBN: 0-307-61938-9 (lib. bdg.)

Are You My Mother? P.D. Eastman. (1960). Beginner Books., Random House.
    ISBN: 0-394-80018-4
    ISBN: 0-394-90018-9 (lib. bdg.)

More, More, More, Said the Baby. Vera B. Williams. (1990). Greenwillow Books, A
    Division of William Morrow & Co., 105 Madison Avenue, New York, NY 10016.
    ISBN: 0-688-09173-3
    ISBN: 0-688-09174-1 (lib. bdg.)

Don't Wake Up Mama! Eileen Christelow. (1992). Clarion Books., A Houghton Mifflin
    Co., 215 Park Ave. South., New York, NY 10003.
    ISBN: 0-395-60176-2

Clean House for Mole and Mouse*. Harriet Ziefert. (1988). Puffin Books., Viking Penguin
    Inc., 40 West 23rd Street, New York, NY 10010.
    ISBN: 0-14-050810-4

Goodnight Moon*. Margaret Wise Brown. (1947). HarperTrophy, A Division of
    HarperCollins., Harper & Row, Publishers, Inc.
    ISBN: 0-06-443017-0 (pbk.)

* Big Books

Family Fun Unit
I.E.P. Goals and Objectives

The child will:

- ❐ identify and express:
    - ❐ his / her name.
    - ❐ family members' names.
    - ❐ classmates' names.

- ❐ identify and express body parts.

- ❐ identify, express, and categorize:
    - ❐ animals.
    - ❐ vehicles.
    - ❐ household room.
    - ❐ household items.
    - ❐ cleaning items.

- ❐ demonstrate emergent literacy skills:
    - ❐ identify beginning sounds.
    - ❐ identify letters of the alphabet.
    - ❐ identify / express rhyming words.
    - ❐ identify picture communication symbols / words.
    - ❐ read a 3-5 word picture communication symbol sentence.
    - ❐ follow a picture communication symbol recipe sequence.
    - ❐ attend to and participate in storytime.
    - ❐ respond to comprehension questions relating to a story.

- ❐ demonstrate pragmatic communication skills:
    - ❐ turn-taking.
    - ❐ requesting reoccurrence; more.
    - ❐ express negation; no / not.
    - ❐ express rote-social exchanges: greetings, farewells, introductions.
    - ❐ label objects / pictures.
    - ❐ respond to "wh" and "yes / no" questions.
    - ❐ indicate a choice.
    - ❐ express wants / needs.
    - ❐ activate a switch to make an action occur.

Family Fun-Related Literature

On Mother's Lap	Ann Herbert Scott
Just Like Daddy	Frank Asch
Peter's Chair	Ezra Jack Keats
A Chair for My Mother*	Vera B. Williams
Goldilocks & the Three Bears	Traditional
Is Your Mama a Llama?*	Deborah Guarino
The Farmer in the Dell*	Mary Maki Rae
Clifford's Family*	Norman Bridwell
Just Shopping With Mom	Mercer Mayer
Just Me and My Dad	Mercer Mayer
Just For You	Mercer Mayer
The New Baby	Mercer Mayer
Runaway Bunny	Margaret Wise Brown
The Three Little Pigs	Traditional
The House That Jack Built	E. Guilfolle
Five Little Monkeys Jumping on the Bed	Eileen Christelow
In A People House	Theo LeSieg
This is a Place for Me*	JoAnna Cole
All About You*	Catherine & Laurence Anholt
Mama, Do You Love Me?*	Barbara M. Joosse
A House Is a House for Me*	Mary Ann Hoberman
Families Are Different*	Nina Pellegrini
Love You Forever	Robert Munsch
Ten, Nine, Eight	Molly Bang

*Big Book

Family Fun - Music Resources

"What Is Your Name?"
"Marching Around the Alphabet"
"The Number March"
"This Is the Way We Get Up in the Morning"

Learning Basic Skills Through Music:Vol. 1
Hap Palmer 1969
Educational Activities Inc.
Box 392
Freeport, NY 11520

"Hello"
"Show Me"

Learning Basic Skills Through Music:
Vocabulary
Hap Palmer 1981
Educational Activities Inc.
Box 392
Freeport, NY 11520

"Rock-A-Bye Baby"

Lullaby Time-for Little People
Kimbo Educational 1975
PO. Box 477
Long Branch, NJ 07740

"Simon Says"
"Rock 'Round the Mulberry Bush"

We All Live Together: Vol. 3
Greg & Steve
Little House Music (ASCAP)
Youngheart Records 1979
Los Angeles, CA 90027

"Goodnight"

Witches' Brew
Hap Palmer 1976
Educational Activities Inc.
Box 392
Freeport, NY 11520

"Hey Diddle Diddle"

Nursery Rhymes
Sing & Learn 1988
Macmillan Educational Co.

Families
Sing & Learn 1989
Macmillan Ed. Co.

Self-Concept
Sing & Learn1987
Macmillan Ed. Co.

Classic Nursery Rhymes
Hap Palmer

Family Fun - Computer Resources

Jokus Faces - Don Johnston
MAC

Create faces through switch activation

Words Around Me - Edmark
MAC/CD-ROM

Body parts, family members, household items

My House - Laureate Learning Systems
Apple, MAC

Furniture, rooms, household items

First Words - Laureate Learning Systems
Apple, MAC, Apple IIe

Household items, body parts

First Verbs - Leaureate Learning Systems
Apple, Apple IIe, MAC

Vocabulary

Exploring First Verbs - Laureate Learning Systems
Apple IIe, MAC, IBM

Vocabulary

First Categories - Laureate Learning Systems
Apple, MAC, Apple IIe

Vocabulary

Exploring First Words - Laureate Learning Systems
Apple IIe, MAC, IBM

Household items, body parts

Bailey's Book House - Edmark
MAC, IBM

Nursery rhymes

Wordwise - Attainment
MAC

People, household items

Touch 'n See - Edmark
Apple IIe

Body parts, household items

Touch 'n Match - Edmark
Apple IIe

Body parts, household items

Reader Rabbit Ready for Letters - The Learning Co.
MAC, IBM

Household items, rooms, furniture

Buddy's Body - UCLA/LAUSD Computer Project
Apple IIe, Powerpad

Body parts

Imagination Express - Edmark
MAC CD-ROM, IBM CD-ROM

People, furniture, rooms

Just Grandma & Me - Broderbund
MAC CD-ROM, IBM CD-ROM

Family-oriented interactive story

All by Myself

by
Mercer Mayer

Summary

In this popular primary storybook, a charming little critter comically demonstrates the things he can do—all by himself.

Children can easily relate to the daily living skills incorporated in the storyline such as dressing, eating, and grooming. Children can also identify with the feelings of pride and self-esteem that come as a result of mastering new skills independently.

Suggested Activities

Sharing the Story

As you read the story, add the repetitive line, "all by myself" after each action. For example, "I can brush my fur, all by myself." Encourage the children to pantomime the actions described in the book. Props could include a critter doll, brush, toothbrush, cup, spoon, truck, pajamas, etc. Let the children choose a prop to use during the story. Use communication overlays on pages 144-147. Read the story again and again. Expand on the theme of the story by using your students' names in the model sentence, "_____can_____ all by himself/herself."

Fun with Music

Lots of children's songs can be adapted to go along with this book. The old favorite, "Mulberry Bush," includes daily living skills that children can act out. You can add your own verses; e.g., "This is the way we use our switch..."

The Hap Palmer song, "Hello" (see Family Fun Music Resources, page 138) also lends itself to gross motor imitation and reinforces social greetings.

What is Your Name?

Sing the song, "What is your Name?" by Hap Palmer, (see Family Fun Music Resources, page 138). Use communication overlays on pages 150-151. Program in the child's name on the right-side location. You can use color photographs instead of the picture communication symbols. This song is great at the beginning of the school year as children are just learning each other's names. You may want to program an overlay with all the student's names on one page and the question, "What is your name?" and use this in morning circle time along with the "Hello" song.

Continued on page 2

Continued from page 1 "What is Your Name?"

For switch activation on a Wolf, program the message, "What is your name?" in the upper left corner location of a grid. Under the yellow cover of the Wolf is a switch plug—it activates this location. This allows the student using the switch to play teacher and ask the other students' their names. See "Wolf Tips," page 14, for directions to turn the switch on.

Critter Capers
Play a game of charades. Duplicate communication overlays on pages 148-149 and cut up into cards. Place the cards face down and have one child pick a card and act out the action from the story. The other children try to guess the action verbally or by using an AC system with the story overlay. Using the props from the story will be helpful. Model the sentence, "I can_____ all by myself," for the children to imitate. Add your own action cards that are personal to your students (wave, drink from a cup, sit down, etc.).

Fun Photos
Take photographs of your students doing things all by themselves at school. Choose skills that they are especially proud of and successful at. All children love to see themselves in pictures. Share the photos with your class and ask them to describe the pictures with a sentence, "___ can ___, all by himself/herself."

The photographs can be copied and blown up to display in your classroom or hallway with the repetitive line written under it. This is very effective for Open House or Parents Night. Parents naturally enjoy seeing what their children can do when they visit school.

Brag Book
Duplicate the photo frame on page 152 for each student. Let the children color in their frame if desired. Glue the Fun Photo from the above activity to the frame. Assemble the pages into a class book and staple. You may want to back each page with construction paper so the book is more durable. Each child can write his/her name and then read his/her page of the class book.
Alternatives:
- Scan the photos into your computer and then print out a class book for every child.
- Make color or black/white copies of each page and then assemble a class book for each child to take home.
- Instead of color photographs, you can use picture communication symbols to depict the actions for the book.

Name Prints

1. Mix playground sand with a colored powder paint in a container. Repeat with different color paint in each container.
2. On construction paper, assist children in printing their first name in large letters.
3. Outline the letters with liquid glue.
4. Let the children choose the colored sand they want.
5. Sprinkle the colored sand over the letters and shake off excess sand. Let dry.

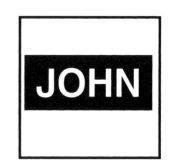

You can use the name prints for props during the song, "What is Your Name?" or you can display them in your room.

Alphabet Names

1. Assist the children in writing their first name on a piece of paper.
2. Give each child a bowl of alphabet cereal.
3. Help the children find the letters of their name in the cereal, using the written model.
4. Glue the cereal letters to a piece of paper.

HINT: You may have to reshape some of the cereal pieces and glue them in place for certain letters.

First Letter Pretzels

1. Thaw frozen bread/roll dough.
2. Give each child a piece of the dough and help him/her roll it out into a long snake.
3. Help each child form the dough into the first letter of his/her name. Provide a large cut-out letter for a model, or write the letter on a piece of paper.
4. Place the bread dough letters on a greased cookie sheet. You can brush the letters with beaten egg whites and sprinkle with coarse salt if desired.
5. Bake as directed and enjoy!

Variation: to make your own dough, use the simple recipe below and duplicate the Letter Pretzel Recipe Strips on page 153 for your students to follow during the activity.

1. Dissolve 1 T. of yeast into 1/2 c. of warm water.
2. Add 1 tsp. of honey and 1 tsp. of salt.
3. Add 1 1/3 c. flour.
4. Knead dough.
5. Roll dough to form letters.
6. Brush letters with beaten egg.
7. Sprinkle with salt.
8. Bake 10 min. at 425 degrees.

Carryover Activities

Pages 154-155

All by Myself!

All by Myself!

I can . . . .

Communication Overlay C - Wolf

All by Myself! 	I can brush my hair. 	I can put on my socks and shoes. 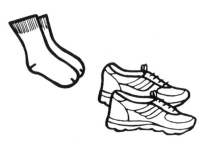
I can eat. 	I can play with my toys. 	I can help Mom and Dad. 
I can put on my pajamas. 	I can brush my teeth. 	I can put myself to bed. 

Communication Overlay D - Macaw

I can brush my hair. 	I can put on my socks and shoes. 	I can eat. 	I can play with my toys.

| I can put on my pajamas.  | I can brush my teeth. 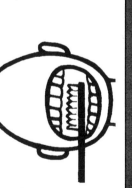 | I can put myself to bed.  | All by Myself!  |

Communication Overlay E - Wolf

I can. . .	get out of bed	All by Myself!
button my overalls	brush my hair	put on my socks and shoes
pour	eat	play with my toys
look	help Mom and Dad	color
put my toys away	put on my pajamas	brush my teeth
put myself to bed	read a story	Goodnight!

Communication Overlay F - Macaw

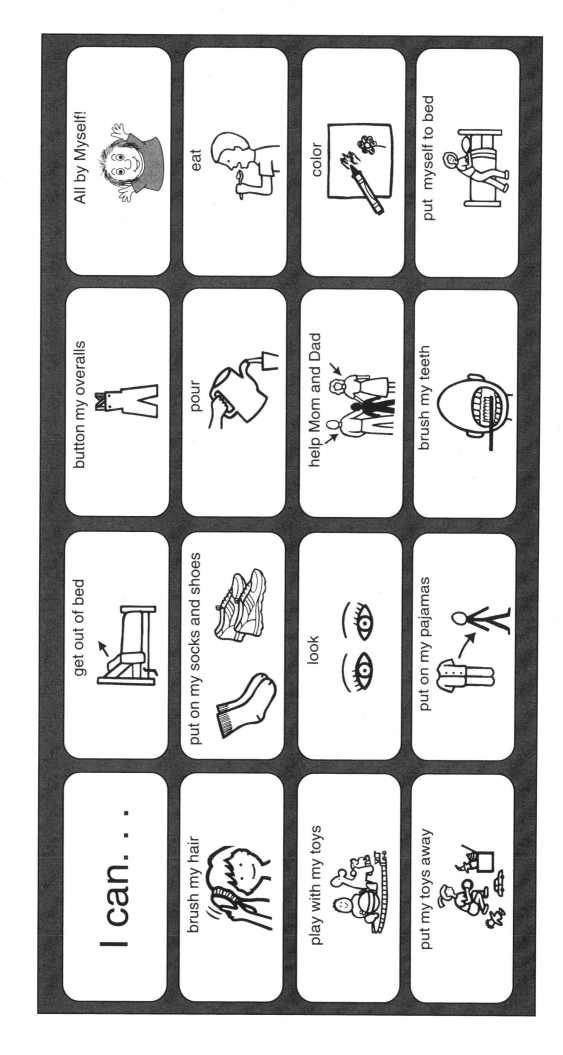

Communication Overlay G - Wolf

What is your name?

My name is:

Communication Overlay H - Macaw

What is your name?

My name is:

Fun Photos

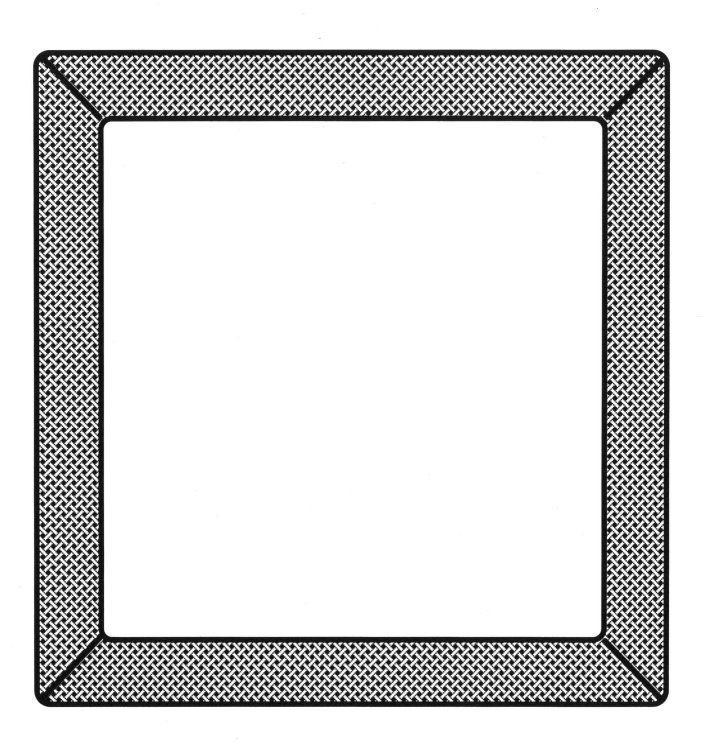

_____ can all by himself/herself.
(name)

Letter Pretzel Recipe Strips

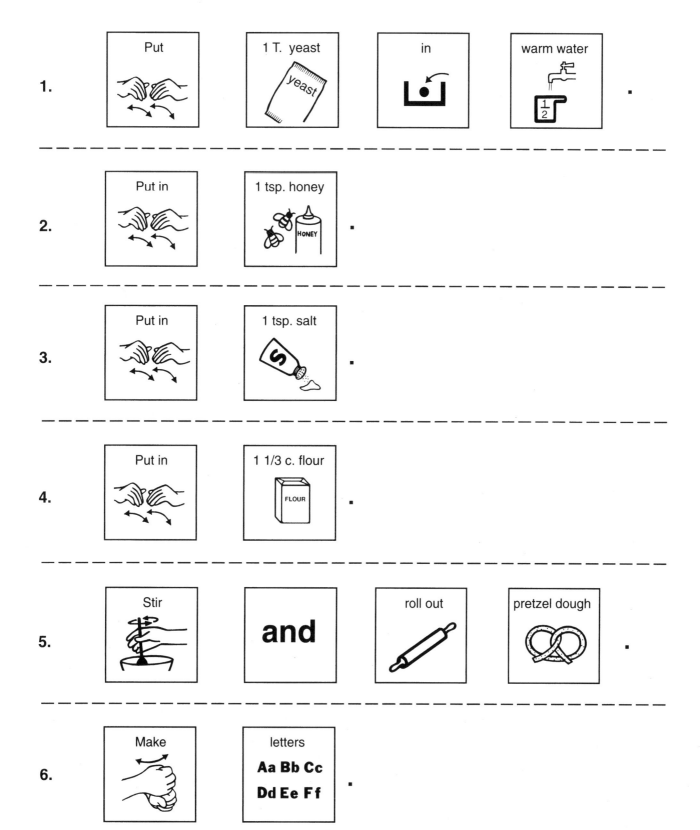

1. Put | 1 T. yeast | in | warm water .

2. Put in | 1 tsp. honey .

3. Put in | 1 tsp. salt .

4. Put in | 1 1/3 c. flour .

5. Stir | and | roll out | pretzel dough .

6. Make | letters Aa Bb Cc Dd Ee Ff .

All by Myself

Match the action to the object by drawing a line.

brush hair

food

put on

clothes

pour

brush

eat

juice

154

All by Myself
Tell Me About It!

1. In the morning, I can _____ all by myself.

eat	go to bathroom	get up	put on

- -

2. At school, I can _____ all by myself.

pick up toys	read a book	be a friend	color

- -

3. On the playground, I can _____ all by myself.

swing	slide	play in the sand

- -

4. At home, I can _____ all by myself.

watch T.V.	brush teeth	drive a car	put on pajamas

- -

1. Cut out into strips if desired.
2. Children can point to or mark correct answer.

Are You My Mother?
by
P.D. Eastman

Summary

A baby bird falls out of his nest and proceeds to look for his mother. As he meets each new character in the story, the baby bird hopefully asks, "Are you my mother?" Finally, the baby bird and the mother bird are reunited in their nest. The cumulative text includes animal and vehicle vocabulary as well as a repetitive line.

Suggested Activities

Sharing the Story

Assemble the story props (items or pictures): mother and baby bird, plastic egg, dog, kitten, transportation items, etc. Let each child choose a prop. Switch-activated toys make wonderful props (a front-loader truck, etc.). Use a battery-switch adapter to make a battery-operated toy, switch-accessible (see page 14 for instructions).

This story is great for working on sentence formation and negation. While sharing the story, ask the students, "Was the dog his mother?" so they can practice using negation (NOT! or No!). Also, have the children repeat the cumulative sequence from the story; e.g. "The dog was not his mother. The kitten was not his mother. The cow was not his mother...," while taking turns using their props.

Choose the communication overlay, pages 160-162, that is appropriate for your students. Program messages from the story: "Are you my mother?" etc. Enjoy and of course read this book again and again.

Family Puppets

Duplicate the family puppet set, page 168, for each child in your class and include a mother, father, brother, sister, and baby. Decorate, color, cut out, and laminate the paper puppets as desired. Attach each puppet to a popsicle or craft stick. Sing, "Where Is Mommy?" (see Fun with Music on next page) using the puppet set. You can customize the symbols so they resemble the child's family. *Variation:* Use real family photos instead of the picture communication symbols. Then you can play a guessing game by holding up a family puppet and asking, "Is this your mother?" The children can practice using the negative, NOT!

Make character puppets from the story by cutting out the picture symbols from the communication overlays provided (bird, kitten, hen, dog, cow) and sing, "Where Is Thumbkin?" with your own lyrics from the story; e.g., "Where is kitty?" "Where is doggie?"

Fun with Music

Sing the song, "'Where Is Thumbkin?" using the following lyrics and the family puppets from the previous activity.

> Where is Mommy?
> Where is Mommy?
> Here I am.
> Here I am.
> How are you today?
> Very well, I thank you.
> Run and hide.
> Run and hide.
> Where is Daddy?...
> Where is brother?...
> Where is sister?...
> Where is baby?...

Birds' Nests

Make rice krispy treats in an electric skillet with your class. Use the recipe strips so children can read the directions on page 169.

1. Melt 1/4 c. butter or margarine in the skillet over low heat.
2. Add 1 (10 oz.) package of regular marshmallows or 4 c. of miniature marshmallows.
3. Stir until completely melted.
4. Add 6 c. of rice krispies.
5. Stir thoroughly.
6. Grease a small bowl (or use muffin tin).
7. Put a scoop of the rice krispy treats in each bowl/cup and press against the sides to form a nest. *HINT:* Grease the students fingers so the mixture won't stick.
8. Let the nests cool until stiff.
9. Remove the nests from the bowl/cup and add jelly beans for bird eggs.

The best part of this activity is eating the nest, of course!

Popcorn Trees

Pop popcorn with your class. Use communication overlays on pages 170-171. (You can connect an air popcorn popper to an environmental control unit for switch activation.) Set popcorn aside. Duplicate the tree outline on page 172 for each student. Color the picture with crayons and then have children apply liquid glue to the inside of the tree. Place popped kernels on the tree for blossoms. You can also glue on jelly beans for bird eggs. Have your students read the picture communication symbol sentence at the bottom of the page.

Variation: Buy colored kernels for popping. Or you can color the popcorn yourself by shaking popped kernels in a plastic baggy with dry powder paint. **Don't let students eat the colored popcorn.**

My Mom
Duplicate the My Mom overlay on page 173 for each child. Let children draw or add facial features to resemble their mothers. They can glue on yarn for hair, raisins, or buttons for eyes, etc. Be creative!

For nonverbal students, this overlay can become a communication grid for the Wolf: duplicate the face overlay and cut it out. Then program the messages in the indicated locations on a 6x6 grid, see page 174 for directions. Students can use this overlay to label facial parts on their pictures or ask you to add the features for them ("Put hair here," "I need a nose"). You can draw or add the facial features while the face overlay is actually on the Wolf! For Macaw users, duplicate the overlay on page 175 and follow the programming directions on the bottom of the page. You can use the copy function on the right half of the page for easier programming.

Animal Lotto
Duplicate communication overlay, page 162 or 164, twice for each child. Color, cut and laminate the picture communication cards so there are two of each symbol. Mix up the cards and place them face down. Let the children play Lotto or a matching game with the characters from the story.

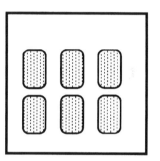

Hide and Seek
Play hide and seek using an AC device. Duplicate communication overlay, page 162 or 164, (Macaw-8 or Wolf-9). Color the overlay and program a Hawk/Wolf or a Macaw to correspond to the picture symbols: "The kitten was not his mother," for the kitten; "The dog was not his mother," for the dog; and "Are you my mother?" for the baby bird. Duplicate the Hide and Seek grid; cut out, align, and glue on top of the communication overlay. Have the student pretend to be the baby bird and try to find his mother by lifting the flap and activating the message under each location. The mother bird could say, "Ah Ha! You found me!" You can play the game again and again by changing the messages and the picture symbols around. *HINT:* For faster device programming, copy the message, "NOT!" or "I am not your mother," in every location except the baby bird and the mother bird location.

Carryover Activities
Pages 176-178

Communication Overlay B - Macaw

Communication Overlay C - Wolf

Hide and Seek - Wolf

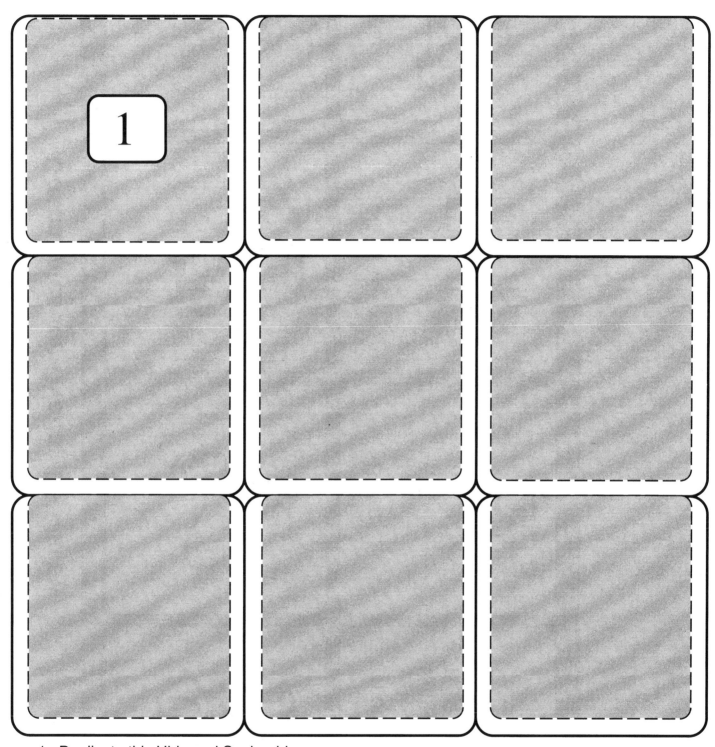

1. Duplicate this Hide and Seek grid.
2. Cut along the dotted lines of the gray squares to make the flaps.
3. Cut out gray square "1" completely.
4. Place grid on top of the Communication Overlay C - Wolf (9 overlay) and align.
5. Glue Hide and Seek grid on top to create flaps.

Communication Overlay D - Macaw

Hide and Seek - Macaw

1. Duplicate this Hide and Seek grid.
2. Cut along the dotted lines of the gray squares to make the flaps.
3. Cut out gray square "1" completely.
4. Glue grid on top of the Communication Overlay D - Macaw (8 overlay) and align.
5. Glue Hide and Seek grid on top to create flaps.

Communication Overlay E - Wolf

mother	egg	jump(ed)
Are you my mother?	kitten	look(ed)
hen	dog	fly
cow	car	stop(ped)
boat	Snort	not
airplane	up	down

Communication Overlay F - Macaw

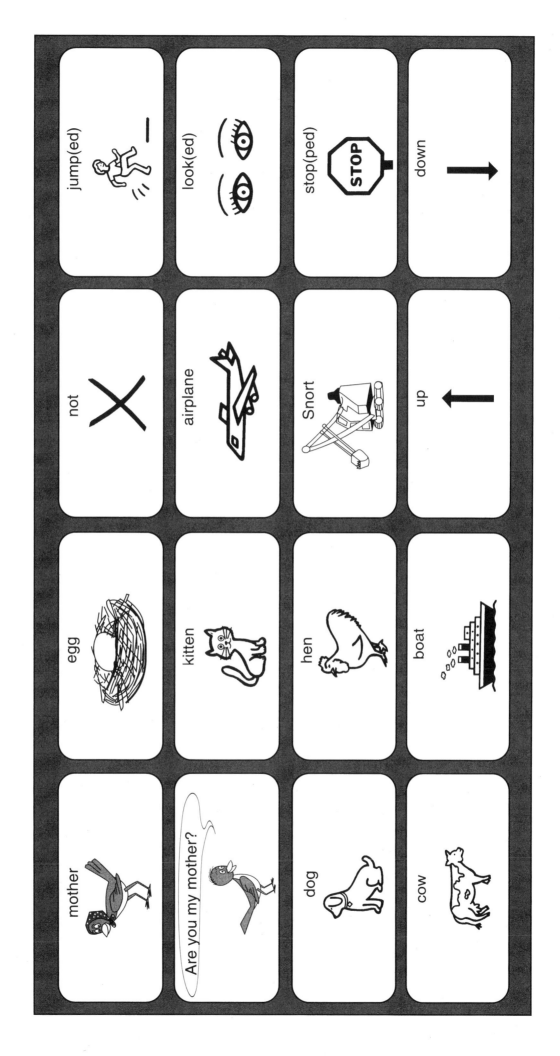

Family Puppets

1. Copy a family puppet set for each child to include mother, father, sister, brother, baby, and . . .
2. Color, decorate, and cut out each family member. Laminate if desired.
3. Attach to a Popsicle/craft stick to make a stick puppet.

168

Birds' Nests Recipe Strips

1. 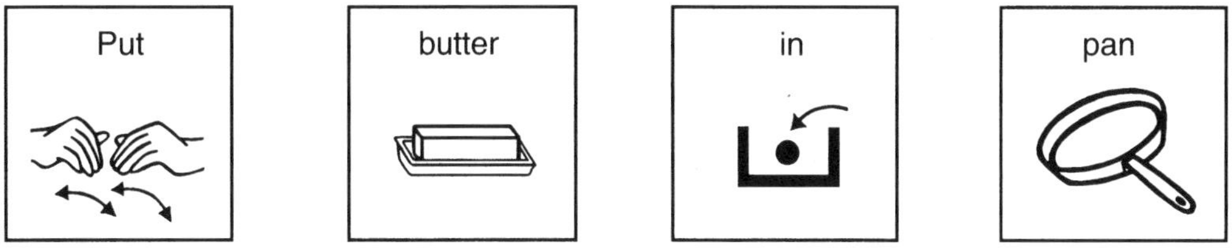 | Put | butter | in | pan |

2. 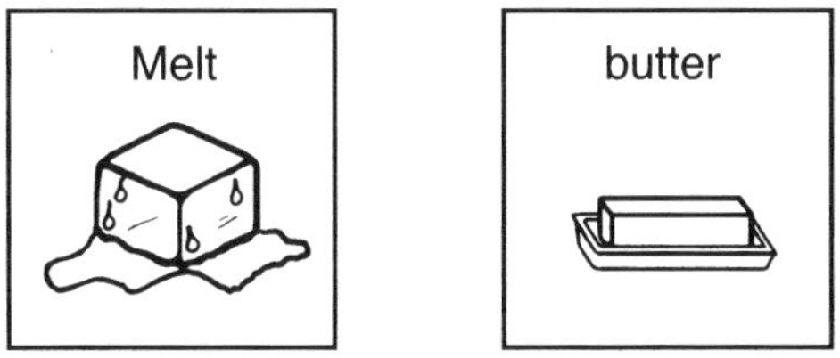 | Melt | butter |

3. 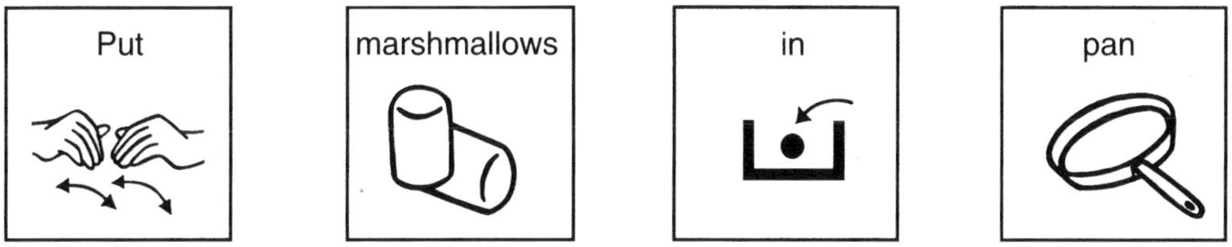 | Put | marshmallows | in | pan |

4. 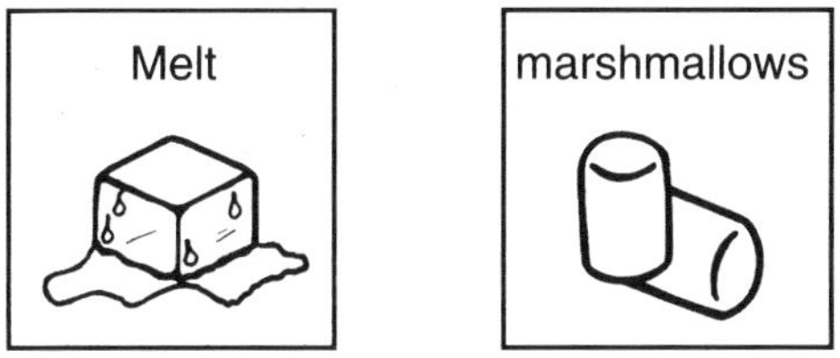 | Melt | marshmallows |

5. 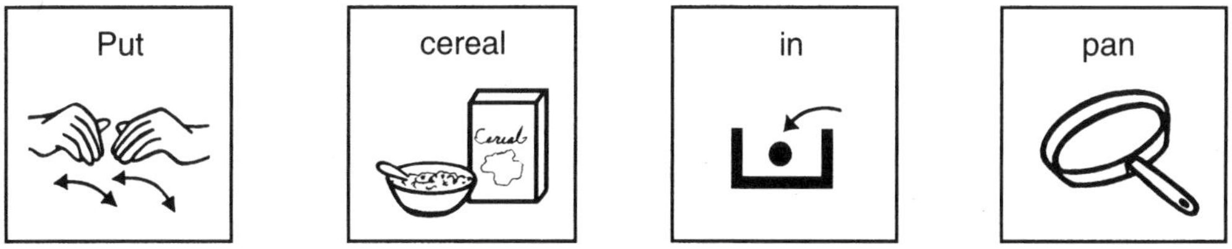 | Put | cereal | in | pan |

6. 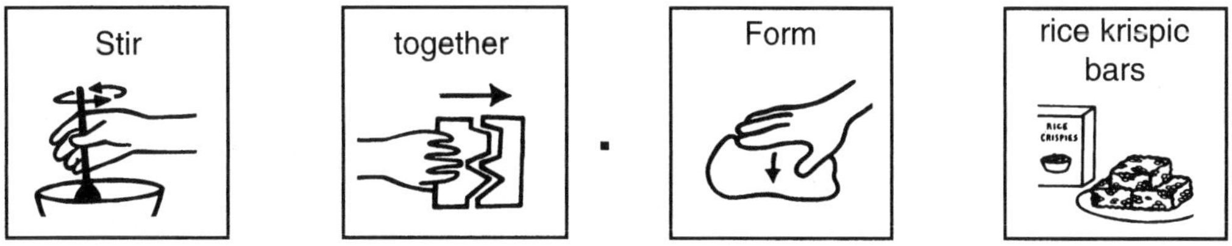 | Stir | together | Form | rice krispic bars |

Communication Overlay G - Macaw

Put in the kernels.

Turn on the popcorn popper.

It's popping!

I want popcorn!

Communication Overlay H - Wolf

Put in the kernels.

Turn on the popcorn popper.

It's popping!

I want some popcorn!

Popcorn Tree

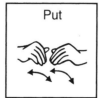
Put

popcorn

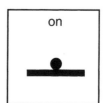
on

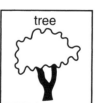
tree

.

172

My Mom - Wolf

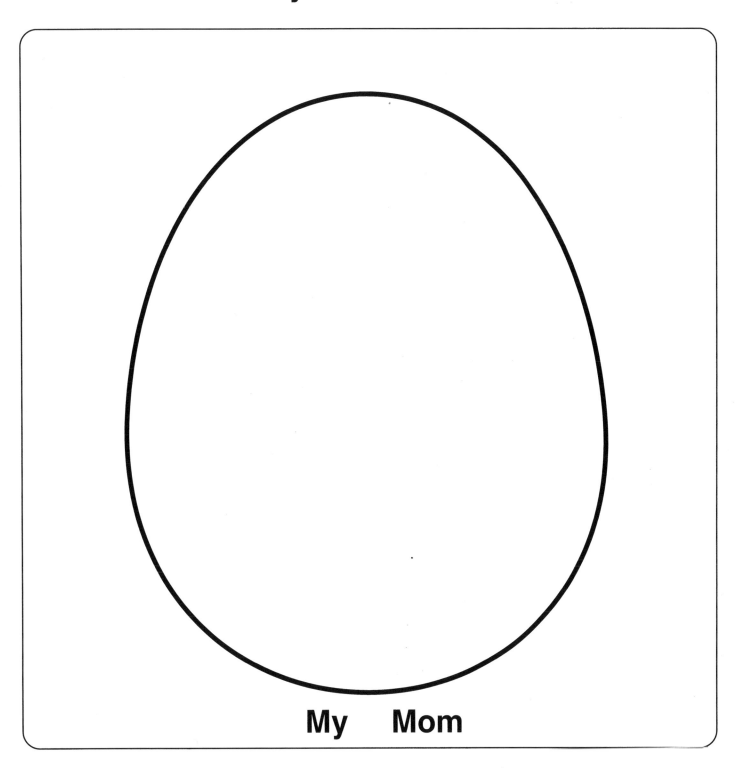

My   Mom

1. Copy and cut out the face overlay to fit the Wolf touch panel.
2. Program a 6 x 6 overlay with facial part messages (see next page).
3. Add facial features to make a picture of mom!

My Mother - Wolf

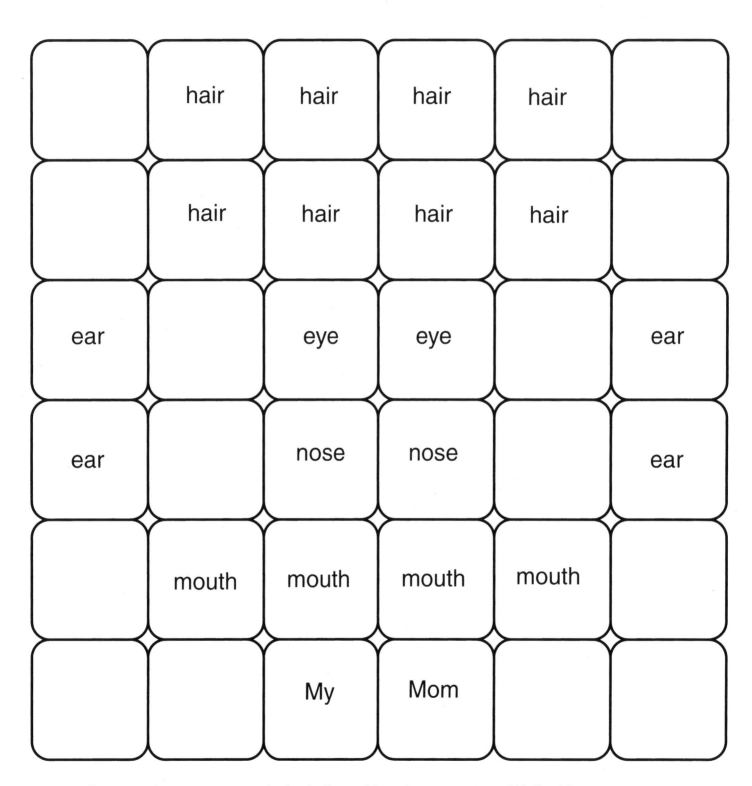

	hair	hair	hair	hair	
	hair	hair	hair	hair	
ear		eye	eye		ear
ear		nose	nose		ear
	mouth	mouth	mouth	mouth	
		My	Mom		

1. Program these messages in the indicated locations on a 6 x 6 Wolf grid.
2. You may want to create your own messages: "Put a nose on my picture, please!" instead of "nose" or "Ouch! You're on my hair!" for "hair."

My Mom- Macaw

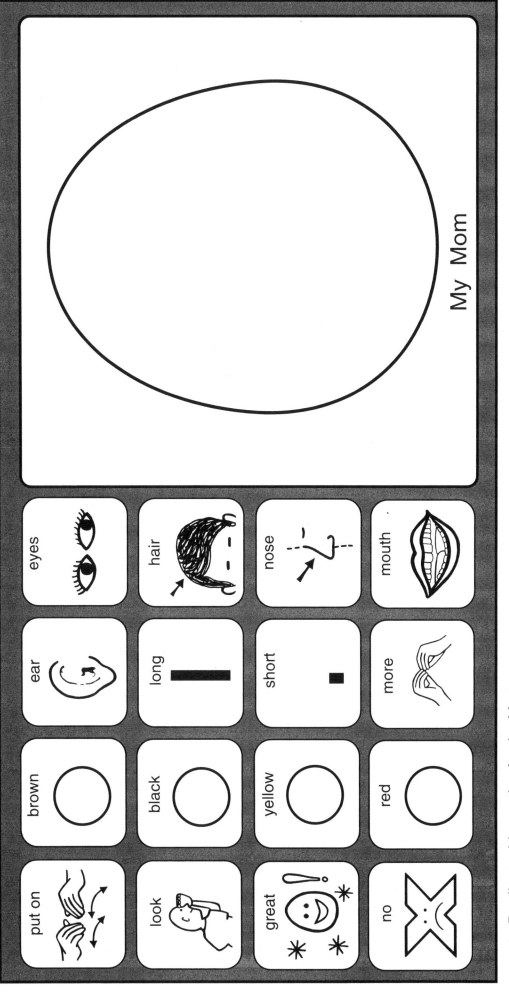

My Mom

1. Duplicate this overlay for the Macaw.
2. Set up a 32 location overlay on the Macaw.
3. Program the facial feature messages on the left half of the grid.
4. Program the message, "here" on the right half of the grid, where the X's are shown. (You can use the COPY function for faster programming.)
5. Students can create sentences such as "Put on brown hair here."

Are You My Mother?

Draw a line to match each baby to its mother.

Category Game - Game Card

Use the picture symbols on the next page to complete the categories.

Category Game - Symbols

1. Copy Category Game Card, page 177, for each child.
2. Have children cut out picture symbols on this page.
3. Glue picture symbols on game card under the correct category.

"More, More, More," Said the Baby

by
Vera B. Williams

Summary

This preschool story beautifully illustrates the love between three families: a father and son, a grandmother and grandchild, and a mother and child. The simple love stories show the adoring adults giving their babies lots of loving attention and the babies yelling for "MORE, MORE, MORE!"

The unique artwork and print in this book are both bold and colorful. The family members represented are multicultural, demonstrating that the universal message of love is shared by all families. This book lends itself to discussing family likenesses as well as differences. Body parts are also highlighted in the text.

Suggested Activities

Sharing the Story

Read the story out loud and use multicultural dolls to represent the family members in the book: father/son, grandmother/baby, mother/daughter, if possible. Or one baby doll could be used for body part identification: belly button, toes, feet, eyes, nose, etc. Have the children take turns tickling or kissing different body parts on the doll as they occur in the book and request, "MORE, MORE, MORE!" Use communication overlays on pages 182-185.

Simon Says

Play Simon Says with your class. Incorporate the body-part vocabulary from the book and a communication overlay (See pages 186-187) for nonverbal students.

The communication overlay on page 188 can be used on a Wolf or a Hawk for students who can directly select a body part on a picture. See page 14-15 for programming suggestions or be creative and make up your own silly messages!

For students who require switch access, program the communication overlay on page 188 using the List Command on a Wolf. (See page 15). Plug a switch into the jack under the yellow cover of the Wolf. Each time the student activates the switch, the Wolf says the messages sequentially, from top to bottom.

Fun with Music
Sing "Rock-a-Bye Baby" (or another favorite lullaby) with your pre-school students. Use a baby doll and a cradle for props. Program a communication device with the lyrics (digitized or recorded speech output is desirable). See overlay on page 190.

More, More, More Game
Practice requesting "More!" during snack time. Program the appropriate communication overlay on page 191 or 192 for your students and/or teach your students the sign for "more." Provide desirable and nondesirable food items (cookies, pickles, lemons, popcorn, juice, etc.). Give children just a taste of a food so they need to ask for more repeatedly.

Variation: Encourage students to request "more," during different activities such as art, music, or storytime. Sabotage the environment by turning off the record player so students have to ask for more, etc.

For switch activation, you can record the simple message, "More, please!" on a loop tape or simple AC device with switch access (Speakeasy, Say-it Switch, Big Mac, etc.).

Funny Footprints
Paint the bottom of your students' feet with washable paint and let them make footprints on construction paper. When the footprints are dry, count the toes and write the numbers 1-10 above them.

Don't forget to play "This little piggy went to market..." while you've got all those toes out! Making up new verses adds to the fun: "This little piggy went to McDonald's, this little piggy stayed home, this little piggy had a Happy Meal, this little piggy had none!"

Look Who's Home
Duplicate the house outline and window frames on pages 193-194 for each child. Discuss each child's family members and let them draw his/her family's pictures in the window frames on page 194. (The PCS family members on page 195 can be used instead of drawings if desired. Color, cut and glue the picture communication symbols onto the window frames on pages 194 to represent each student's family.) Cut on the dotted lines of the house outline to form lift-the-flap windows. Glue or staple the house outline on top of the window frame pictures. Write the names of the family members on the window flaps. Let the children share their work with each other and practice reading the sentence below the house.

Variation: Use real photographs of each child's family. Cut out the photos so they can be glued onto the window frames.

Family Category Game
Display items belonging to different family members: baby bottle, diaper, razor, purse, cane, etc. Help children to identify and name the items as well as categorizing them into groups: baby, father, mother, grandparent.

Duplicate the family category game on pages 196-197 for each child. You can have children draw their own pictures as well as using the PCS provided.

Have children glue the PCS onto the grid. Program a 32-location Macaw overlay with messages that correspond to the items (baby's, mom's, dad's, grandmother's; toys, razor, etc.). Or you may simply choose to program a 4-location page with the messages: "That's baby's," "That's mom's," "That's dad's," and "That's grandma's."

Carryover Activities

Page 198

Communication Overlay C- Wolf

Communication Overlay D- Macaw

Communication Overlay E- Wolf

Simon
Says. . .

Communication Overlay F- Wolf

Simon Says. . .	touch your head	wave your hand
touch your arm	touch your belly/button/ stomach	touch your elbow
touch your fingers	touch your feet/toes	touch your leg

1. Program the messages above in the indicated locations on a Wolf/Hawk 3 x 3 grid.
2. Duplicate the corresponding baby outline on page 186 and place on the touch-panel of the AC device.
3. Play Simon Says with your class.

Communication Overlay G - Wolf

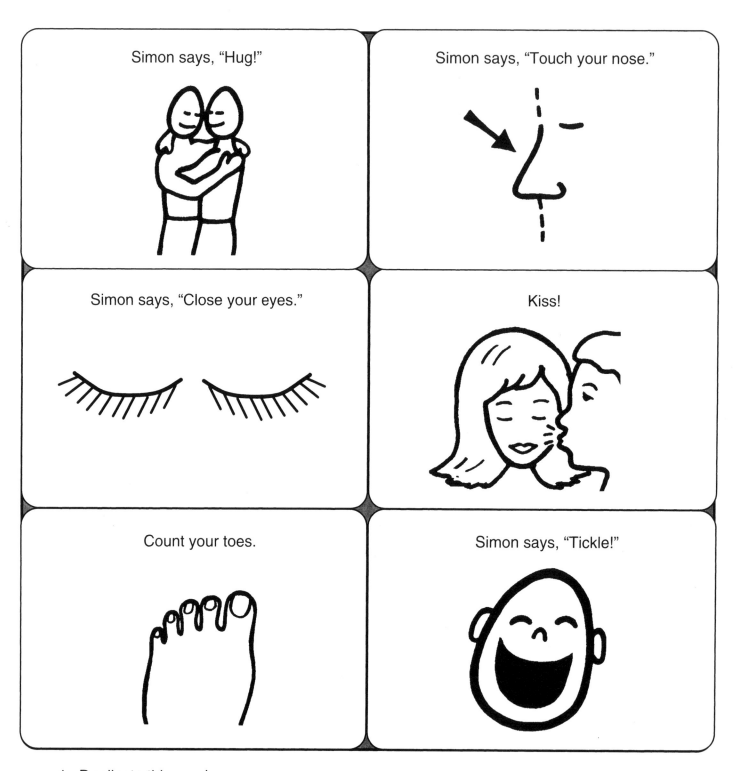

Simon says, "Hug!"

Simon says, "Touch your nose."

Simon says, "Close your eyes."

Kiss!

Count your toes.

Simon says, "Tickle!"

1. Duplicate this overlay.
2. Program the messages on a 2 x 4 location Wolf grid.
3. For switch activation, program these messages as a data page and use the List Command (see Introduction page 15).

Communication Overlay H- Macaw

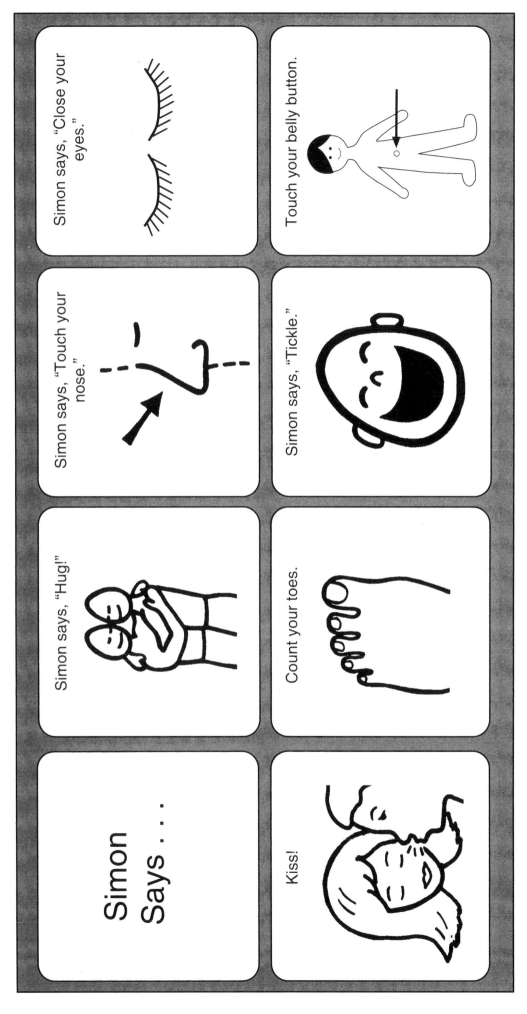

Simon says, "Close your eyes."

Touch your belly button.

Simon says, "Touch your nose."

Simon says, "Tickle."

Simon says, "Hug!"

Count your toes.

Simon Says . . .

Kiss!

1. Duplicate this overlay.
2. Program the messages on an 8-location Macaw grid.
3. Play Simon Says with your class.

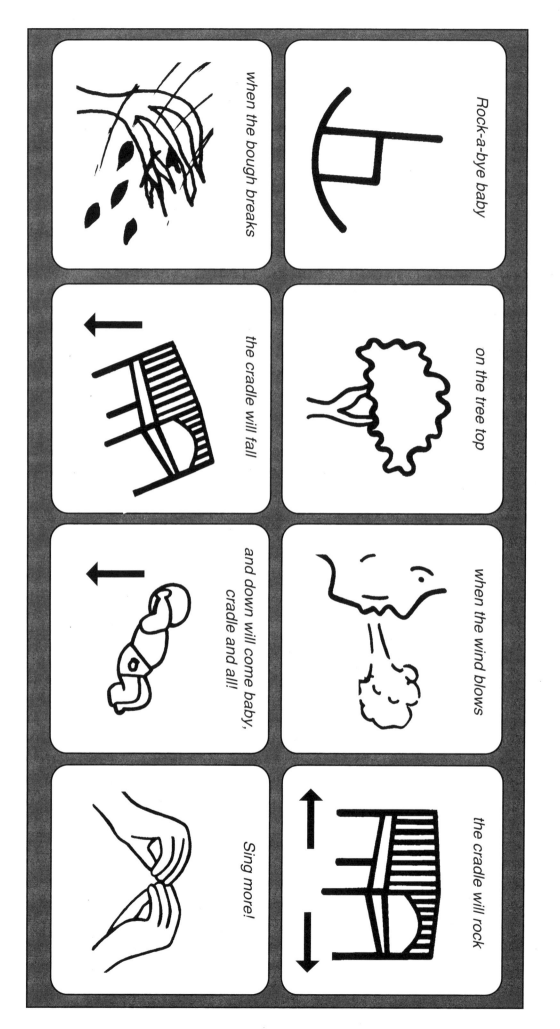

Communication Overlay I- Macaw

more

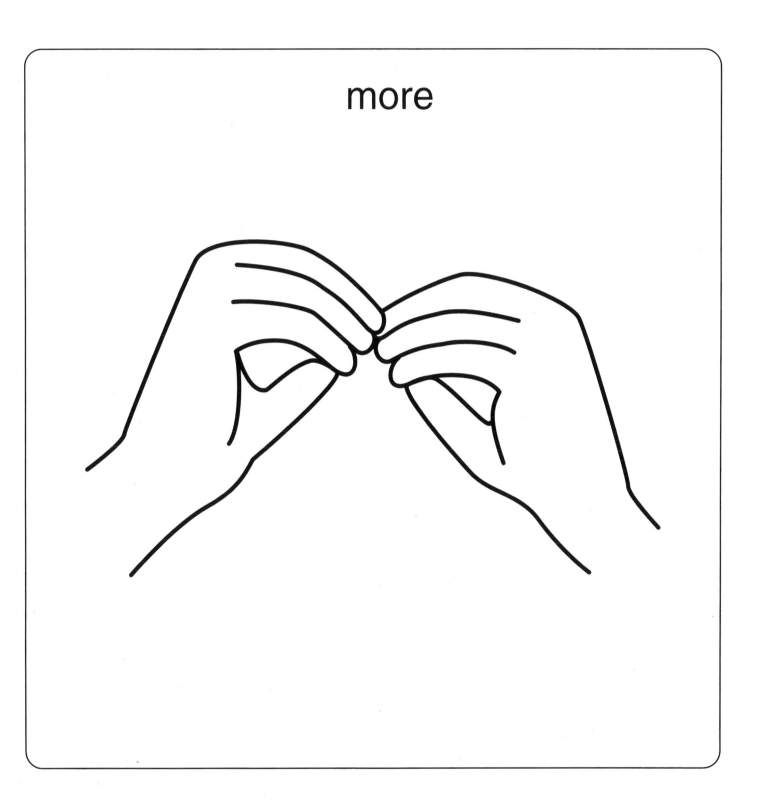

Communication Overlay K - Macaw

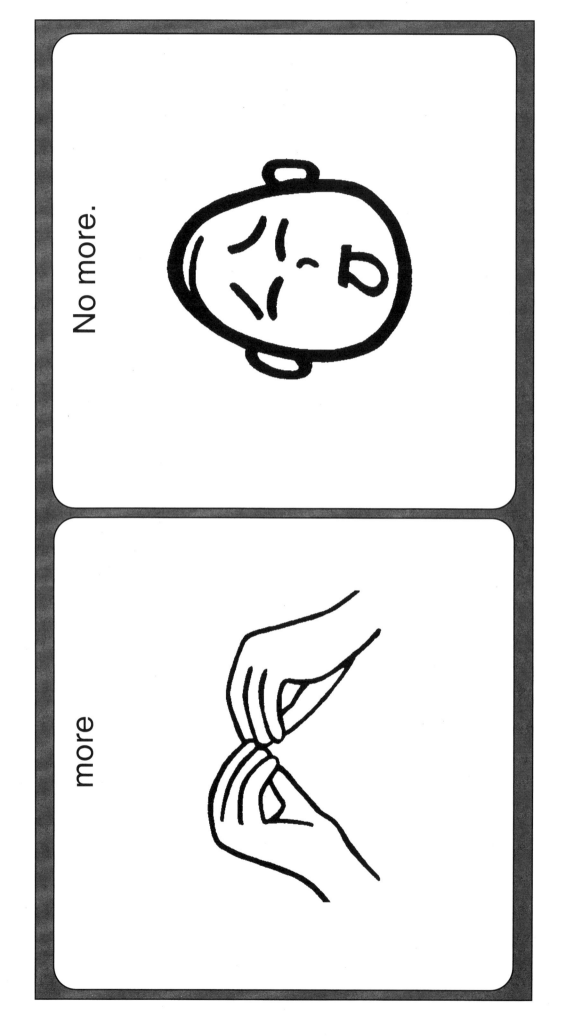

more

No more.

Who's Home?

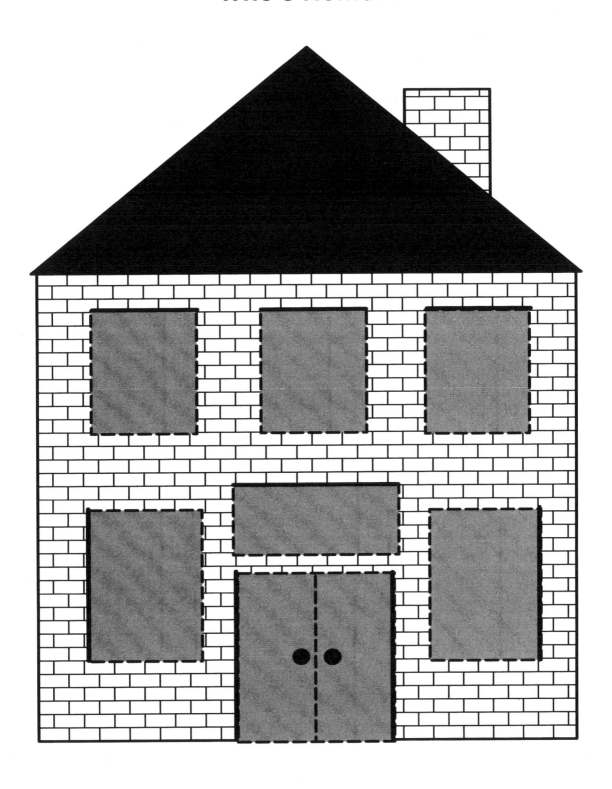

_____ is my .

Window Frames

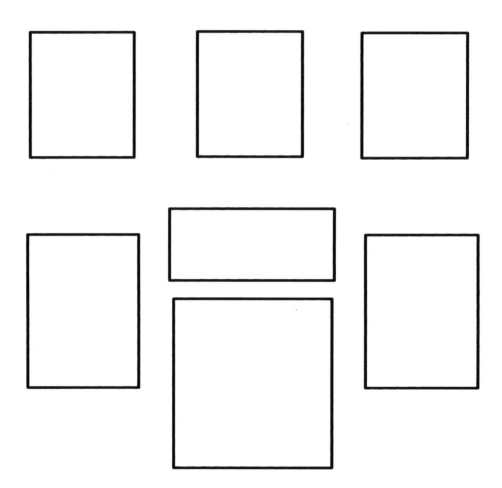

PCS Family Members

1. Duplicate the house outline on page 193 for each child.
2. Cut out the windows and door on the dotted lines to form flaps.
3. Add family members to the window frames on page 194.
4. Glue the house outline on top of the window frames.

Family Category Game - Macaw

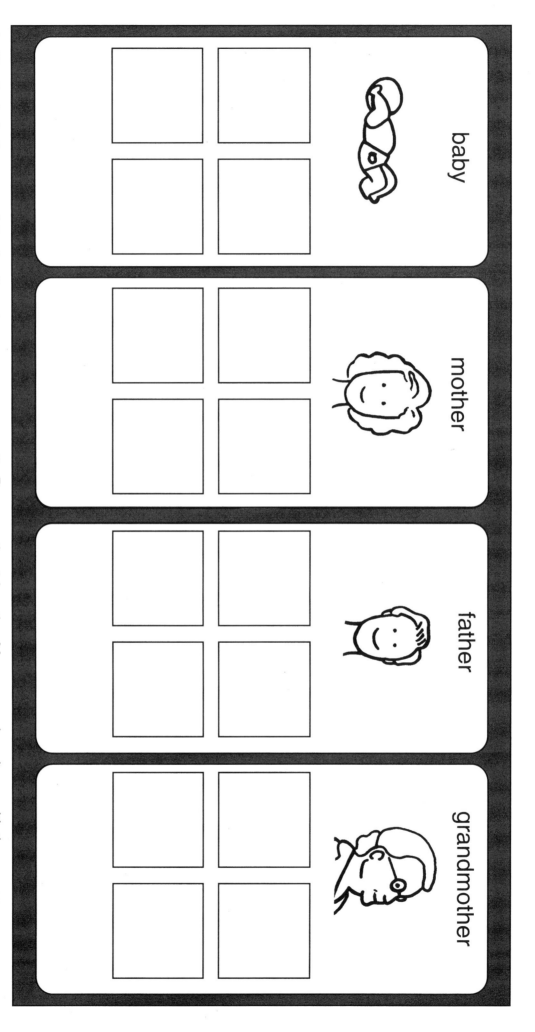

baby

mother

father

grandmother

1. Duplicate both pages of the family category game.
2. Cut out the family items on p. 197 and paste them in the correct column.

3. Program the 4-location Macaw overlay above with the messages: "That's the baby's." "That's mother's." "That's dad's." "That's grandma's."
4. Or program a 32-location Macaw with the item names: tie, dress, toys, etc.

Family Category PCS

Use the symbols below with the Family Category Game, page 196.

cane	suit	shoe
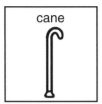		

baby carriage	necklace	dentures
	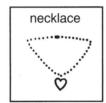	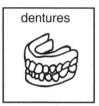

glasses	dress	razor

toys	briefcase	diaper

lipstick	tie	crib
		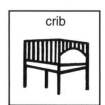

More, More, More!
Tell Me About It!

1. What did Little Guy do?

run   cry   drink

- -

2. What did Little Guy's Daddy do?

run   kiss   eat

- -

3. Which one is Little Guy?   Little Pumpkin?   Little Bird?

- -

4. What do you like more of . . .?

kiss   hug   work   sleep

1. Cut out into strips if desired.
2. Children can point to or mark correct answers.

Don't Wake Up Mama

Another Five Little Monkey's Story
by
Eileen Christelow

Summary

The five little monkeys (infamous for jumping on the bed) are up to mischief again! In this delightful story, the monkeys attempt to bake a birthday cake for their mother without waking her up. The plot heats up as two firefighters arrive on the scene to discover the burned cake. Lots of frosting patches things up for a happy ending.

Suggested Activities

Sharing the Story

This story is especially fun to read with your class during a birthday celebration. Cooking utensils (mixing bowl, measuring cup/spoons, recipe book, and cake ingredients), along with monkey puppets are natural props for this story.

Children love to bang utensils and then scold each other with the repetitive line, "Don't wake up Mama!" Take turns role-playing the characters. You can use a firefighter's hat for the firefighter. Don't forget to sing "Happy Birthday" at the end of the book. Use the communication overlays that are best suited to your students' needs, pages 202-207.

Five Little Monkeys

Teach your class the finger play, "Five Little Monkeys Jumping on the Bed." Make the five little monkeys stick puppets on page 209 and duplicate the bed outline on page 208 for each student. Insert the monkey puppets into the bed and remove one monkey at a time while reciting the familiar rhyme. You can also read the book *Five Little Monkeys Jumping on the Bed* by Eileen Christelow with your class.

Fun with Music

All children enjoy singing "Happy Birthday." Sing the song with your class and use communication overlays on pages 210-211. We suggest programming the "'Happy Birthday" song on an AC device with digitized or recorded speech (Macaw, Hawk, etc.). *NOTE:* For Wolf users, the birthday song is preprogrammed on the Wolf CAP: Beginning Level.

Birthday Cake

Bake a birthday cake with your class using a prepackaged mix (unless of course you're as daring as the five little monkeys!).

Plug an electric mixer into an environmental control unit along with a switch to provide switch access if needed. Provide a communication overlay to go along with this activity, page 212 or 213. Program a Wolf using the List command for switch activation (see page 15 for instructions).

While the cake is baking, let the children color canned vanilla frosting by adding a few drops of food coloring and stirring. Then they can choose different color frostings to spread on their cake. Add decorations as well: sprinkles, candy hearts, M&Ms, etc.

Variation: Use a microwave cake mix or cupcake mix if you're in a hurry. Or simply provide the children with prebaked cupcakes to frost and decorate. Each child can count the number of candles for his/her cake and add to the top. All children love to blow out candles.

Birthday Card

Let your students design their own birthday cards. Provide each child with a piece of construction paper (folded in half to form a card), markers, crayons, and/or paint. Let them add decorations (glitter, stickers or stamps.) and dictate or write a message. The birthday cake outline on page 214 can be duplicated, cut out, and glued on the front of the card if desired.

Ideas: • cotton or cotton balls for frosting on a cake
  • glitter on the candles
  • sprinkles, M&Ms, hearts, etc.
  • squares of wrapping paper for presents

Variation: Many computer programs contain card making activities. Try **Bailey's Book House** by Edmark or **Print Shop**.

Counting Candles

Duplicate the birthday cake outline and the birthday candles on pages 214-216 for each child. Help the children identify their age and count the corresponding number of candles needed for their cake. The children can then color the candles and the cake outline. Assist them in cutting out the candles and gluing them to the top of the birthday cake outline. They can also cut out the number and glue it on the sentence for shared reading.

Variation: Use real birthday candles for counting practice, and let the children put them into their own birthday cupcake or glue onto the cake outline on page 214.

Monkey Masks

Give each child a paper plate (dinner or desert size). Let them color the entire plate brown and then add facial features with crayons or markers. Use the monkey symbol next to this activity for a model. You can glue yarn on the top for hair and glue on construction paper ears. The eyes and/or the mouth can be cut out to form a mask. The monkeys can then be glued to craft sticks to make paper-plate puppets or attach yarn/string for masks.

Use these monkeys for props while reading a five little monkeys story.

Pin the Tail on the Monkey

Play pin the tail on the monkey with your class for a birthday party. Duplicate the monkey outline and tail on pages 217-218. You can enlarge the outlines if desired. Color, cut out, and laminate the monkey parts. You may want to back the pieces with tag board or construction paper for added durability. Hang up the monkey in your classroom and let children take turns trying to pin on his tail.
NOTE: Enlarge the picture of the monkey tail if desired.
Variation: You can mount the monkey on a flannel board or tray and hold it up to make it easier for physically challenged students.

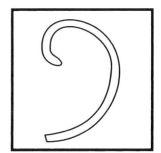

Carryover Activities

Pages 219-220

Communication Overlay B - Macaw

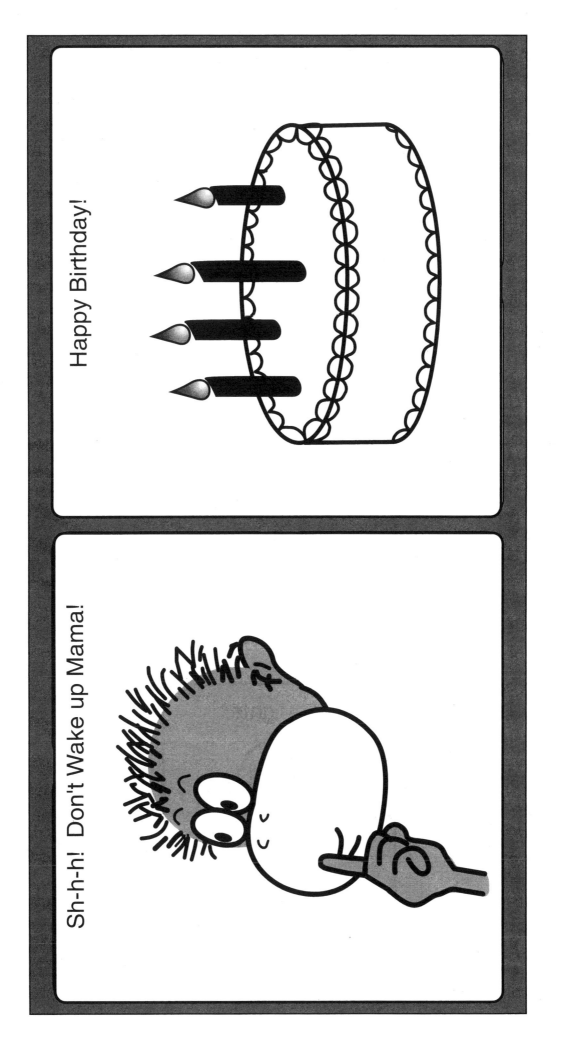

Communication Overlay C- Wolf

Shh! Don't wake up Mama! 	5 little monkeys 	Let's bake a cake! 
Read the recipe. 	Mama's asleep! 	present 
Oh no! 	firefighter 	Happy Birthday! 

Communication Overlay D- Macaw

Communication Overlay E - Wolf

Shh! Don't wake up Mama!	5 little monkeys	Mama's asleep!
Let's bake a cake!	Read the recipe.	flour and baking powder 2 c. 3 tsp.
4 eggs	sugar and oil	mix
Put it in the oven.	present	Turn off the oven!
firefighter	frosting	Oh no!
ahh-choo!	Happy Birthday. . .	eat

Communication Overlay F - Macaw

Shh! Don't wake up Mama!	5 little monkeys	Let's bake a cake!	Read the recipe.
Mama's asleep!	flour and baking powder	4 eggs	sugar and oil
mix	Put it in the oven.	present	firefighter
frosting	ahh-choo!	Oh no!	Happy Birthday . . . .

Five Little Monkeys Jumping on the Bed!

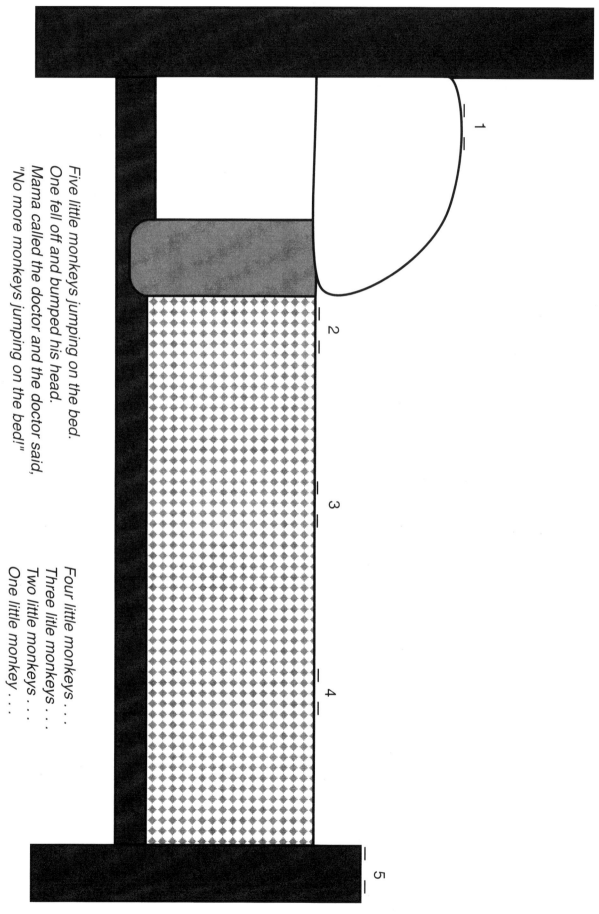

Five little monkeys jumping on the bed.
One fell off and bumped his head.
Mama called the doctor and the doctor said,
"No more monkeys jumping on the bed!"

Four little monkeys . . . .
Three little monkeys . . . .
Two little monkeys . . . .
One little monkey . . . .

Five Little Monkeys Jumping on the Bed!

1. Duplicate, color, and cut out the five little monkeys above.
2. Glue a craft or Popsicle stick to the back of each monkey.
3. Cut 5 slits on the bed outline (as indicated) and insert the monkey puppets.
4. Glue the edges of the bed outline to construction paper for backing.
5. Remove the monkeys as you read the rhyme.

Communication Overlay H- Macaw

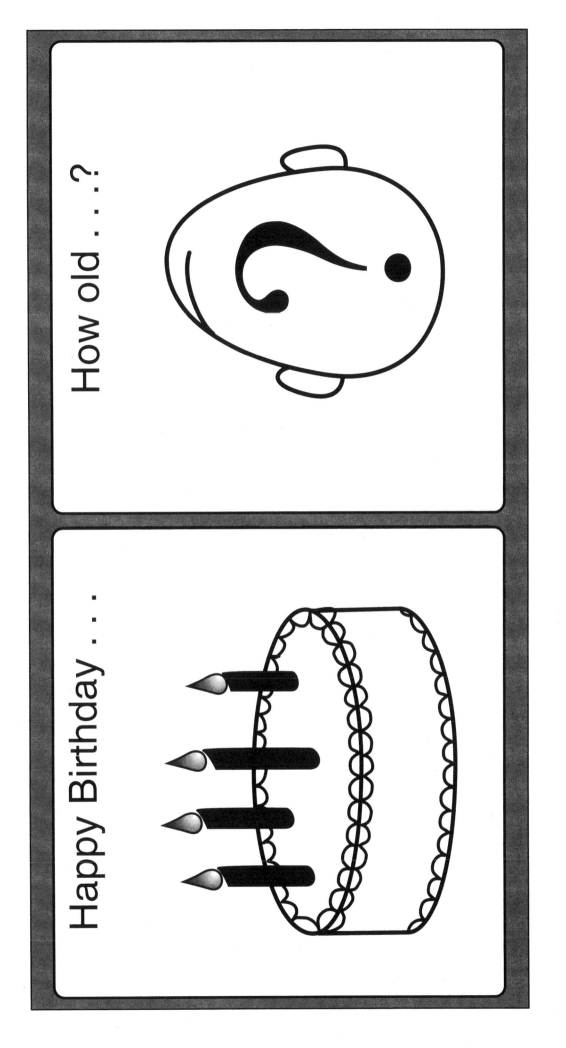

Happy Birthday . . .

How old . . . ?

Communication Overlay I - Wolf

Put in the cake mix.

Put in the oil.

Put in the eggs.

Turn on the mixer.

Put in the water.

Put the cake in the oven.

NOTE: (Program using list command, see p15).

Communication Overlay J - Macaw

Put in the cake mix. 	Put in the eggs. 	Put in water. 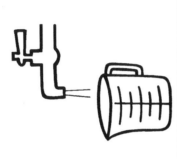	Put in the oil. 
Turn on the mixer. 	Put the cake in the oven. 	I need frosting. 	My turn.

I am _____ **years old.**

Don't Wake Up Mama!
Birthday Candles

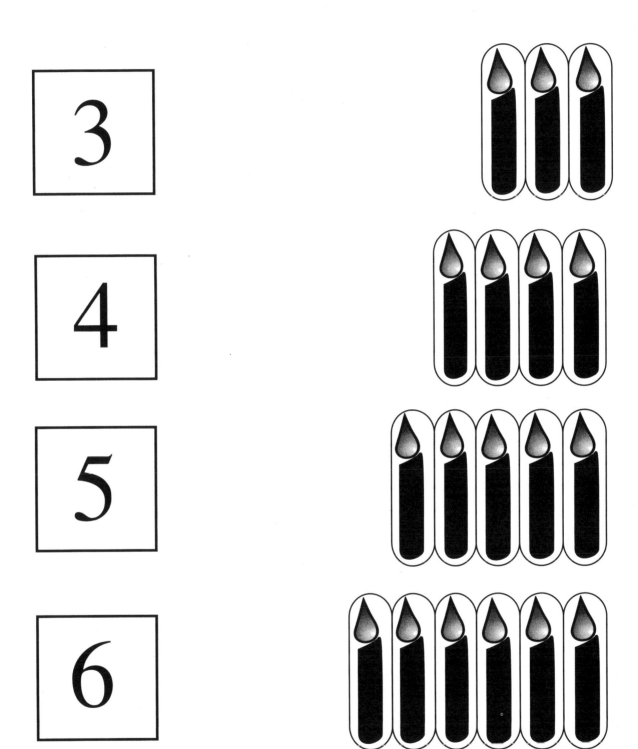

1. Cut out the age and matching number of candles for each child.
2. Glue the candles to the top of the birthday cake on page 214.
3. Glue the number on the sentence line.
4. Have the children read their sentence!

Don't Wake Up Mama!
Birthday Candles

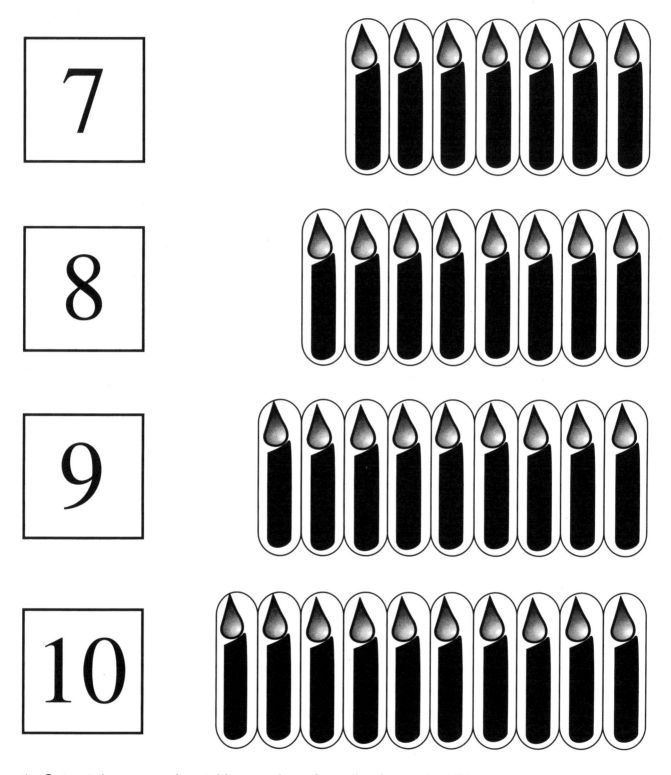

1. Cut out the age and matching number of candles for each child.
2. Glue the candles to the top of the birthday cake on page 214
3. Glue the number on the sentence line.
4. Have the children read their sentence!

Pin the tail on the monkey

Pin the tail on the monkey

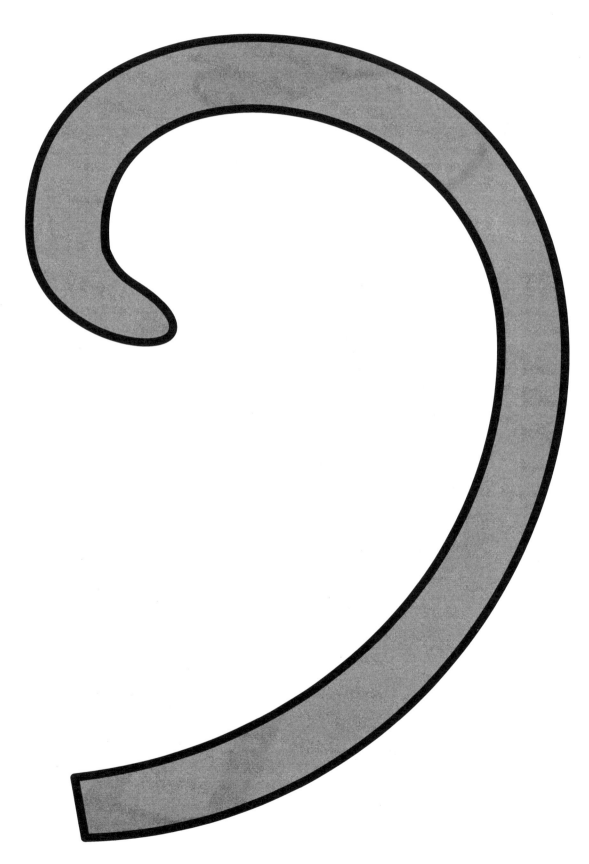

Don't Wake Up Mama!
Cake Matching

Draw a line to the matching cakes.

Don't Wake Up Mama
Tell Me About It!

1. What did the little monkeys make?

hamburger 	cake 	orange juice 	present 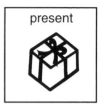

- -

2. How many little monkeys were there?

- -

3. Whose birthday was it?

firefighter 	baby 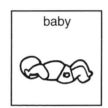	cat 	mama 

- -

4. What was Mama doing?

sleep 	drink 	brush hair 	drive 

- -

5. Who ate the cake?

firefighter 	dog 	monkey 	bug 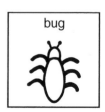

1. Cut out into strips if desired.
2. Children can point to or mark correct answers as teacher reads the question.

220

A Clean House for Mole and Mouse
by
Harriet Ziefert

Summary

Mole and Mouse clean their house so every room looks "just fine." In order to keep their house clean, they shower, sleep, and eat outside!

The simple text in this book contains a repetitive line and emphasizes the concepts of clean and dirty as well as household parts and vocabulary.

Suggested Activities

Sharing the Story

This book is available in a Big Book format which is preferable for reading to a large group of children. Cleaning items such as a broom, dustpan, bucket, sponge, mop, washcloth, etc., make excellent props. Have the children identify, express, and demonstrate the use of the cleaning items during the story. Discuss the rooms of a house and how you clean them. Use a communication overlay during storytelling (see pages 224-229).

Fun with Music

Sing "Mulberry Bush" with the following lyrics and utilize cleaning items for props during the song: broom, dish cloth, mop, etc.

> *"This is the way we clean our house, clean our house, clean our house. This is the way we clean our house so early in the morning.*
> > *"This is the way we sweep the floor..."*
> > *"This is the way we wipe the table..."*
> > *"This is the way we make the bed..."*
> > *"This is the way we wash the windows..."*
> > *"This is the way we mop the floor..."*

Where Does it Go?

Display household items: a doll house with toy furniture or pictures of household items. Help children categorize the items by placing them in groups according to which room they would be found in a house: bedroom, living room, kitchen, bathroom, etc. You can duplicate the room picture symbols used on page 227 to provide visual cues for sorting.

Copy the "Where Does It Go" game on pages 230 and 231 for each student. Students can cut out and glue the picture communication symbols in the correct rooms.

Choosing Chores
Enlist your students' help with classroom cleanup. Let your students choose a job for the day or week by pointing to a picture symbol. Duplicate the Picture Communication Symbols for classroom chores on page 232, or create your own symbols specific to your classroom. Color, cut out, and laminate the symbols cards. Attach a piece of Velcro® to the back of each card and a matching piece of Velcro® next to each student's name on a job chart.

You can create a job chart by listing the students' names on the left side of a piece of chart paper or poster board. As students select a job, they can find their name and place their card next to it. Display the job chart in your classroom.
Idea: A classroom chore for the physically challenged student might be to plug a vacuum cleaner or dust buster into an environmental control unit and attach a switch. Let the student turn the vacuum cleaner on by pressing a switch while another student vacuums.

Graham Cracker Houses
Cut graham cracker squares in half diagonally to form 2 triangles. Leave some of the graham crackers in square form. Have each child identify and choose one square and one triangular graham cracker. Ask them to make a house using their crackers. Use communication overlays on pages 233-234.

Students can spread peanut butter, cream cheese, or marshmallow fluff on their houses and then decorate with sprinkles or candies. Eat and enjoy!

House Stamps
Assemble square and triangular shape sponges, washable paint, shallow tins, and construction paper. Pour a small amount of different colored paint into each tin. Have the students dip the square sponge in the paint and then stamp it on a piece of construction paper. Repeat this process with the triangular sponge to add the roof of the house. Use communication overlays on pages 233-234.
HINT: You can purchase sponges that come in different shapes or simply cut your own sponge before it is wet. Children's bath blocks work well too. For an easier grip, you can hot-glue a dowel or handle to the sponge or block.

Community Carryover

Plan a trip to the grocery store with your class to purchase cleaning items. Use the picture communication symbol shopping cards provided on page 235 and add your own symbols. Cut out the cards and place in a pocket-sized communication wallet. At the store, let the children match the items on their shopping card to the actual cleaning items on the shelf.

Variation: Create a picture shopping list using magazine/newspaper ads. Glue 1-2 pictures on an index card for each child.

Make and Take Storybook

Duplicate the "Make and Take" storybook on pages 236-241 for each child. Let the children identify the household items in each picture and then color the picture. Be sure to read the symbol sentence at the bottom of each page. Staple the pages together to make a book and send home with each student.

Carryover Activities

Pages 242-243

It looked just fine!

Communication Overlay B - Macaw

Mole and Mouse cleaned . . . . .

and the _____ looked just fine.

Communication Overlay C- Wolf

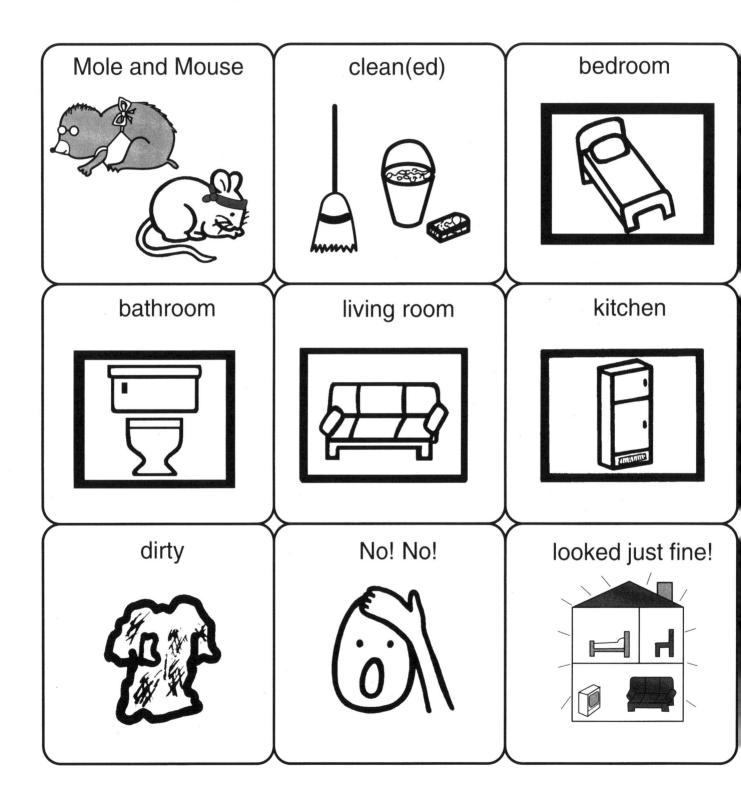

Mole and Mouse	clean(ed)	bedroom
bathroom	living room	kitchen
dirty	No! No!	looked just fine!

Communication Overlay D- Macaw

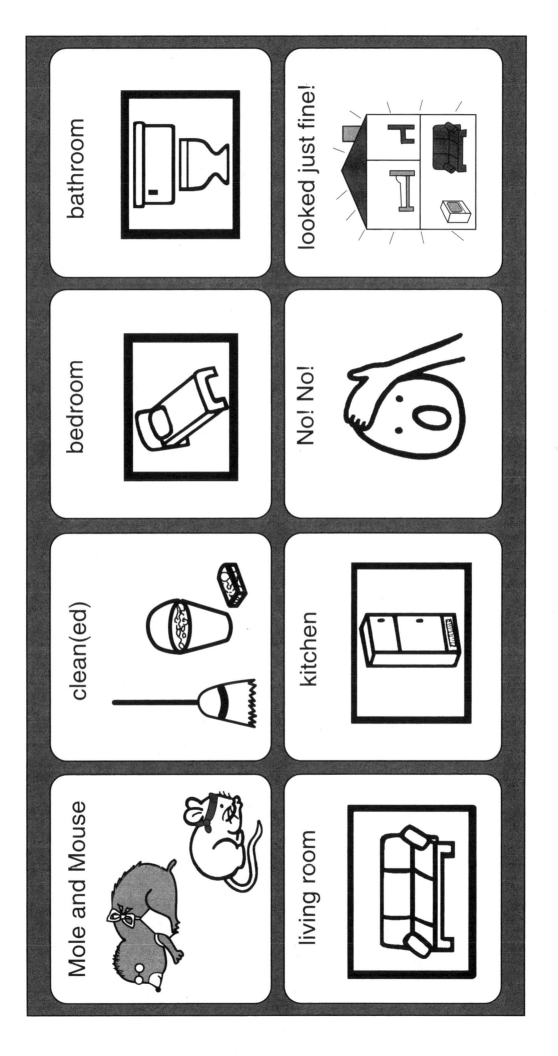

Mole and Mouse

clean(ed)

bedroom

bathroom

kitchen

No! No!

looked just fine!

living room

Communication Overlay E - Wolf

Mole and Mouse	dirty	house
clean(ed)	bedroom	bathroom
living room	kitchen	wash windows
mop	cook	bathe
take a nap	go outside	shower
picnic	Oh no!	looked just fine!

Communication Overlay F - Macaw

house	dirty	clean(ed)	Mole and Mouse
kitchen	living room	bathroom	bedroom
go outside	take a nap	bathe	cook
looked just fine!	Oh no!	picnic	shower

Where Does it Go?

A [bedroom] has

A [bathroom] has

A [kitchen] has

A [living room] has

1. Cut out the household items on page 231 and place in the correct room above.
2. Read the fill-in-the-blank sentences.

Where Does It Go?
Room Items

bed

sink

couch

bathtub

stove

pillow

table
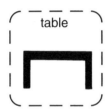

television

chair

refrigerator

toilet

dresser

Classroom Chores

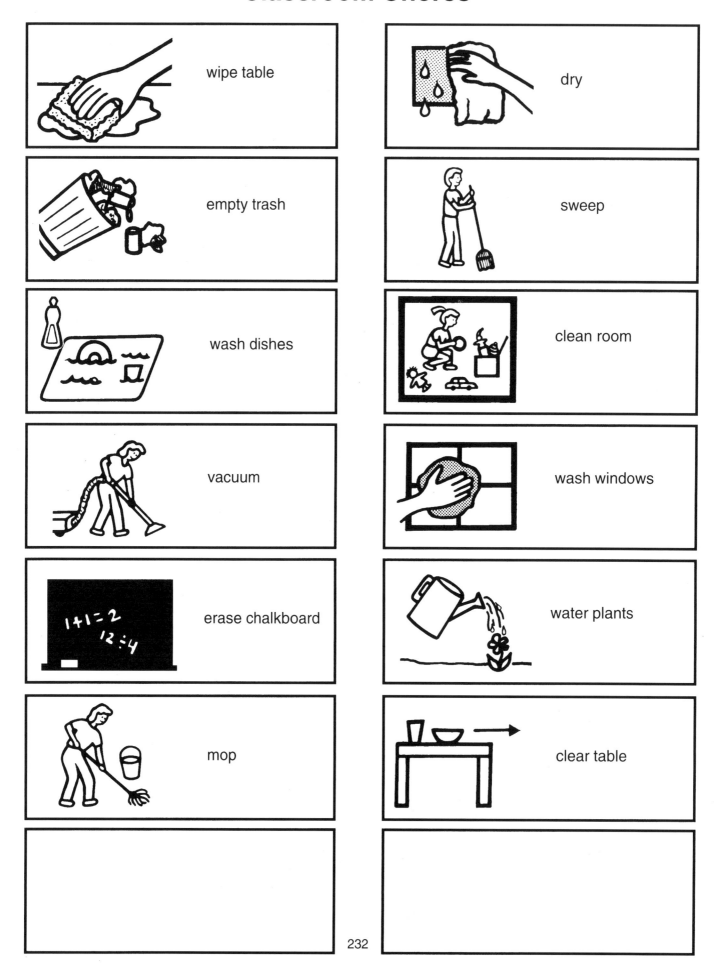

wipe table

dry

empty trash

sweep

wash dishes

clean room

vacuum

wash windows

erase chalkboard

water plants

mop

clear table

Communication Overlay G - Wolf

square

triangle

Look at my house!

I want some!

Communication Overlay H -Macaw

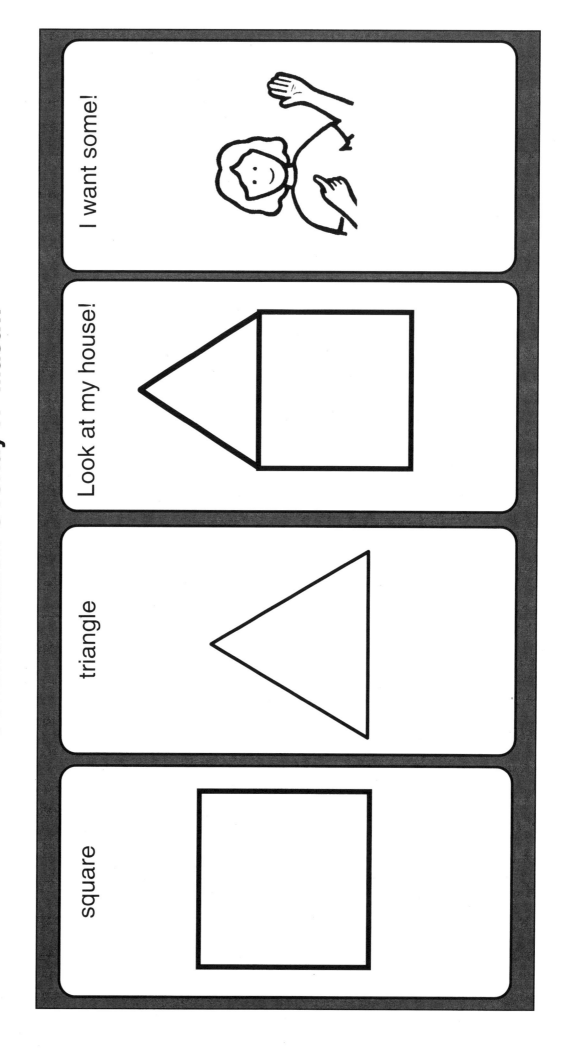

| square | triangle | Look at my house! | I want some! |

Shopping Cards

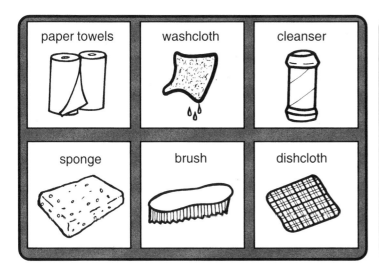

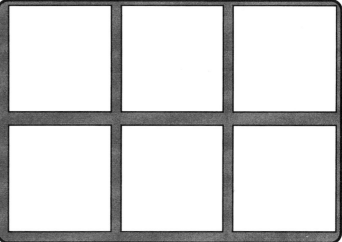

Make & Take Storybook
Cover

Make & Take Storybook
Page 1

| Mole & Mouse | cleaned | the | bedroom |

Mole & Mouse | cleaned | the | bathroom

Mole & Mouse	cleaned	the	living room

Make & Take Storybook
Page 4

Mole & Mouse	cleaned	the	kitchen

Make & Take Storybook
Page 5

It looked just fine

Cleaning Match Up

Match the cleaning items on the left to the household items on the right.

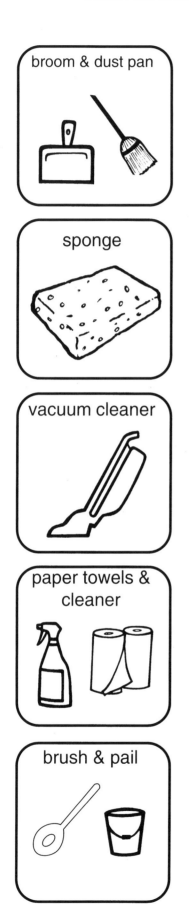

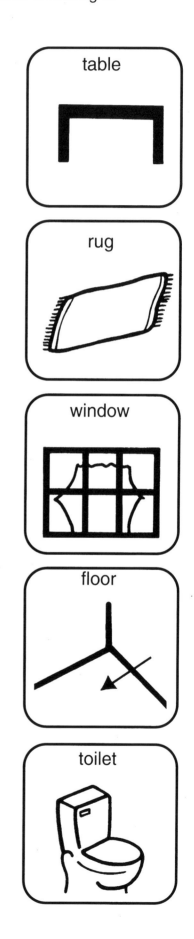

A Clean House for Mole & Mouse
Tell Me About It!

1. Mole and Mouse cleaned their . . .

yard

house

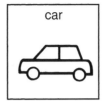
car

clothes

- -

2. Mole and Mouse cleaned the . . .

bathroom

classroom

dining room

bedroom

- -

3. Which room do you sleep in?

bedroom

bathroom

kitchen

- -

4. Which room do you eat in?

bedroom

bathroom

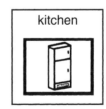
kitchen

- -

5. Which room do you take a bath in?

bedroom

bathroom

kitchen

1. Cut out into strips if desired.
2. Children can point to or mark correct answers.

Goodnight Moon
by
Margaret Wise Brown

Summary

In this popular bedtime classic, a baby bunny bids good night to everything in his bedroom. The artwork is rich in color and vividly illustrates the household items featured in the rhyming text.

Suggested Activities

Sharing the Story

This book is available in a Big Book format as well as paperback. A plush bunny and the items in the bedroom can be used for props during storytime. Have the children repeat the storyline, "Goodnight _____," as the bunny gets ready for bed. Using communication overlays on page 248-251, let children take turns "reading" the story.

Fun with Music

Teach your class a bedtime lullaby. Sing the tune "Goodnight Ladies," using your students' names; e.g., "Goodnight *Susie*, Goodnight *Susie*, Goodnight *Susie*, it's time to go to bed!" This is most appropriate preceding nap or rest time. You can program a communication overlay with the message, "Goodnight" in one location and the students' names in the other location or use the overlay on pages 249.

Variation: Sing the song with the vocabulary items from *Goodnight Moon; e.g.,* "Goodnight, moon...," and use communication overlays on pages 250-251.

Pajama Party

Plan a pretend pajama party with your class. Have the children bring their pajamas to school along with their favorite stuffed animal and bedtime story. (Teachers: Don't forget to wear your P.J.'s too!) Read bedtime stories together; turn off the lights and sing "Goodnight _____" from the activity above. You can pop popcorn and watch a movie before "bed."

HINT: Children love to play with flashlights; bring some to the pajama party just for fun!

Making Mush
Prepare prepackaged instant oatmeal with your class. Let each child choose a packet of oatmeal, open it, and pour it in a bowl. Add hot water as directed. Let the children stir and enjoy! Use communication overlays on pages 256-257, and follow the directions for scanning at the bottom of the page.
Variation: Use instant grits instead of oatmeal.

Nursery Rhymes
Teach your students the popular nursery rhymes Twinkle, Twinkle, Little Star, overlay on page 259; Star Light, Star Bright, overlay on page 261; Hey Diddle, Diddle, overlay on page 263.

Duplicate the dot-to-dot overlays on pages 258 and 262; let children complete the pictures and take home for carryover.

Goodnight Sky Mobile
Create a sky mobile by making salt-dough cutouts in the shapes of stars and a moon. Let each child mix:
    4 TBSP flour
    1 TBSP salt
    2 TBSP water
Knead dough to form a ball. Roll out the dough and use cookie cutters to cut out the star and moon shapes. (A crescent moon can be cut out of a circle shape.) The dough recipe makes 2-3 ornaments (double as needed). Use a straw to poke a hole near the top of each shape--string or yarn can be attached later. Place dough shapes on a cookie sheet and bake at 350° for approximately 30 minutes. When the shapes are cool, let the children decorate with paint or glitter. Attach yarn to the top and hang from a coat hanger (cut string different lengths).
Variation: Make cutout cookies in the shape of stars and moons for snack time.

Musical Alphabet
Sing "Marching Around the Alphabet" by Hap Palmer (see Music Resources on page 138). Place large letter cards on the floor in a circle; children move around the circle until the music stops. They then pick up the letter in front of them and identify the letter and the beginning sound. For switch activation, connect your record player and a switch to an environmental control unit. Then a student can control the music through switch activation. Program an alphabet overlay to correspond to the letter cards for AC users.

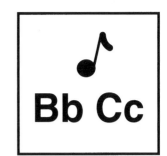

Duplicate the Letter Boxes Game for each student on pages 265-266. For beginning-sound practice, let children cut and paste the Picture Communication Symbols (page 266) and place in the correct Letter Box (page 265).

Carryover Activities

Page 267

Goodnight!

Communication Overlay B - Macaw

Goodnight!

Communication Overlay C- Wolf

Goodnight!	room	telephone & red balloon
	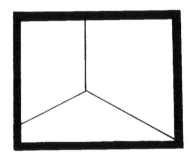	
cow jumping over the moon	3 little bears sitting on chairs	2 little kittens and a pair of mittens

little toy house and a young mouse	comb, brush, and a bowl of mush	quiet old lady whispering "hush"

Communication Overlay D- Macaw

Goodnight!

room

cow jumping over the moon
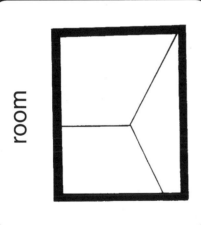

3 little bears sitting on chairs

2 little kittens and a pair of mittens
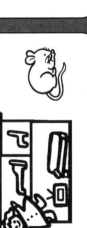

little toyhouse and a young mouse

comb, brush, and a bowl of mush
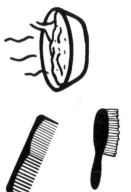

quiet old lady whispering "hush"

Communication Overlay E - Wolf

Goodnight

1. Duplicate and color this overlay for a Wolf.
2. Program the messages (see page 253) on a 3 x 3 location Wolf grid.
3. This becomes a talking overlay that can be used during storytime or for individual play.

Communication Overlay E (messages) - Wolf

Goodnight!	curtain, stars and moon	Cow jumping over the moon
toy house	socks and mittens	bed
table and light	mouse	kitten

Communication Overlay F - Macaw

Goodnight

1. Duplicate and color this overlay for a Macaw.
2. Program the messages (see page 255) on a 32 location Macaw grid.
3. This becomes a talking overlay that can be used during storytime or for individual play.

Communication Overlay F - (Messages) - Macaw

bears	bears	balloon	moon & stars	curtain	cow jumping over the moon	cow jumping over the moon	Goodnight!
bed	bed	bed	light	curtain	fireplace	fireplace	
bed	bed	bowl of mush	a comb & a brush	mittens	socks	fireplace	
bed	bed	kitten	mouse	rug	rug	toy house	toy house

Communication Overlay G - Wolf
Making Mush

Open oatmeal.

Pour in hot water.

Pour oatmeal in a bowl.

Stir.

1. Program this overlay on a 2 x 2 location Wolf grid.
2. For switch activation, program this overlay as a data page and follow the list command directions on page 15 of the Introduction.

Communication Overlay H - Macaw
Making Mush

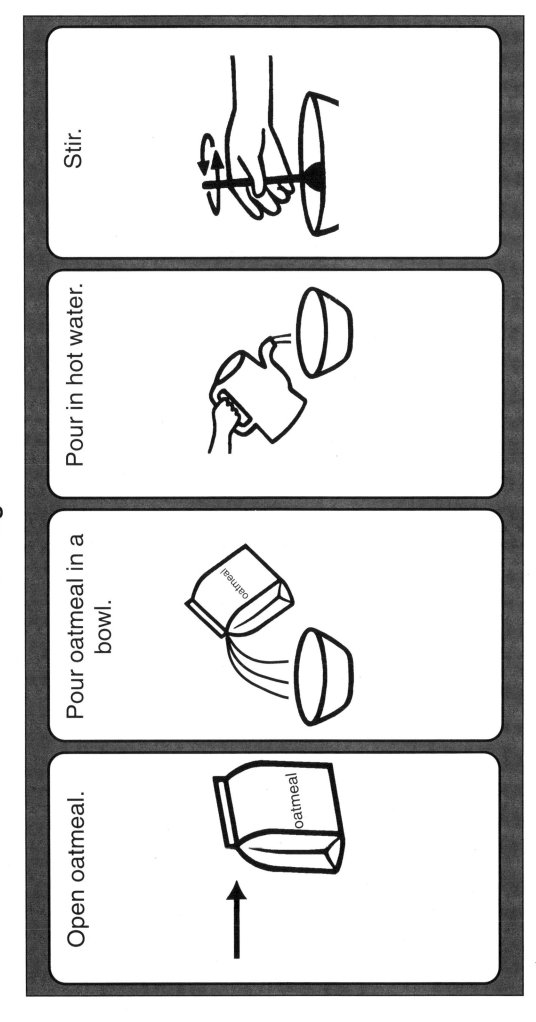

| Open oatmeal. | Pour oatmeal in a bowl. | Pour in hot water. | Stir. |

1. Program this overlay on a 4-location Macaw grid.
2. For switch activation, select the step-scan function in the "record mode" and connect a switch to the switch plug, on a scan-Macaw.

Communication Overlay I - Wolf
Twinkle, Twinkle, Little Star

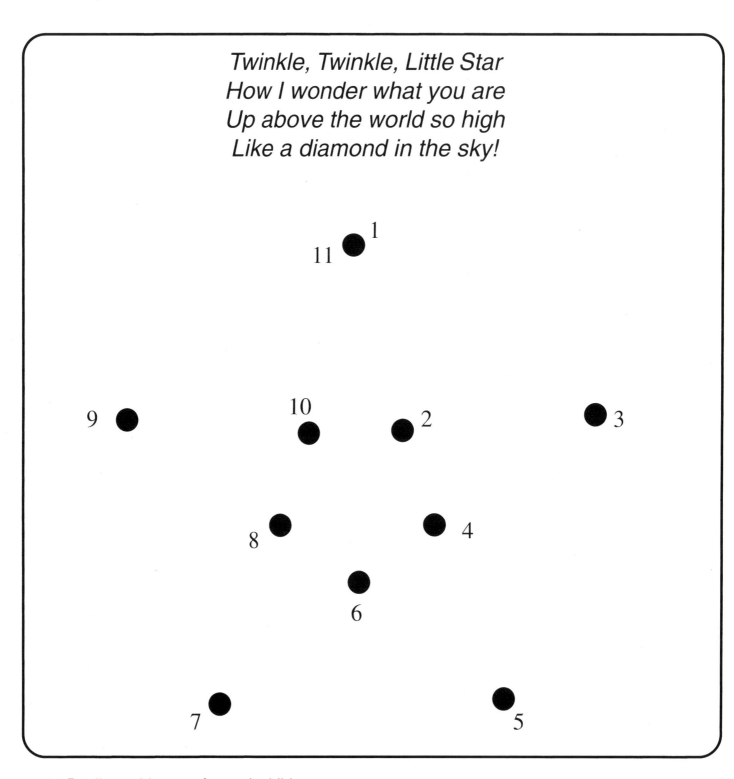

Twinkle, Twinkle, Little Star
How I wonder what you are
Up above the world so high
Like a diamond in the sky!

1. Duplicate this page for each child.
2. Assist them in completing the dot-to-dot star. Color if desired.
3. Program the nursery rhyme into a 1 x 1 Wolf grid and use the dot-to-dot star as the overlay.
4. Send the page home for carryover.

Communication Overlay J - Macaw
Twinkle, Twinkle, Little Star

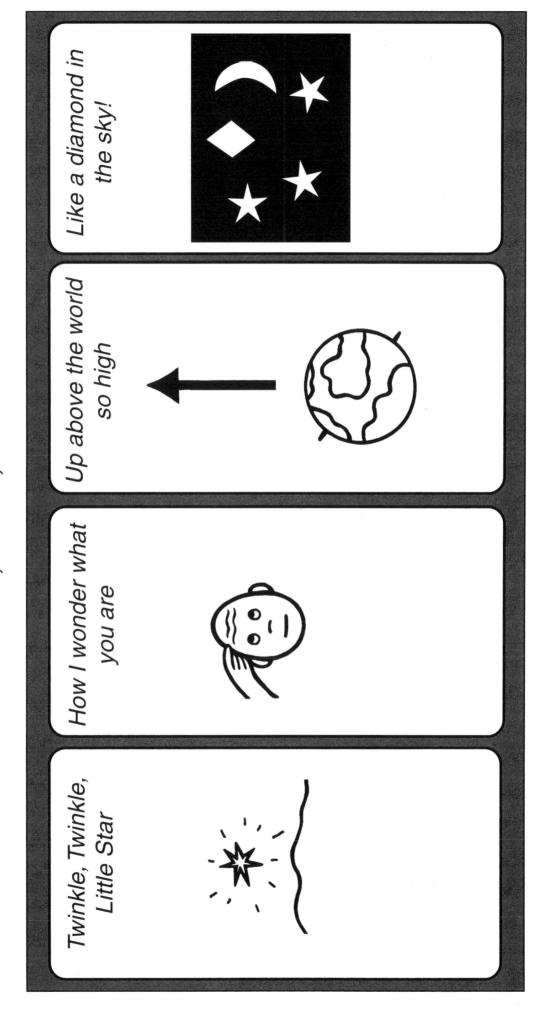

Communication Overlay K - Wolf
Star Light, Star Bright

Star Light
Star Bright
First star I see tonight
I wish I may
I wish I might
Get the wish I wish tonight.

1. Duplicate this page for each child.
2. Have the children apply liquid glue on the stars and moon.
3. Shake on gold or silver glitter and let dry.
4. Program the rhyme on a Wolf 1 x 1 grid and use the glittery overlay.

Communication Overlay L - Macaw
Star Light, Star Bright

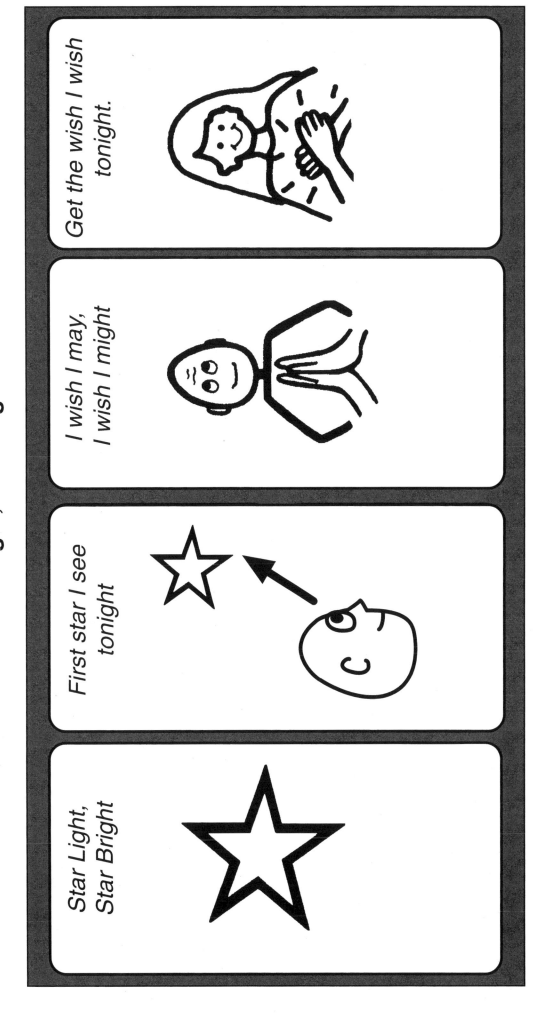

Star Light, Star Bright

First star I see tonight

I wish I may, I wish I might

Get the wish I wish tonight.

Communication Overlay M - Wolf
Hey Diddle Diddle

Hey Diddle Diddle
the cat and the fiddle.
The cow jumped over the moon.
The little dog laughed to see such sport.
And the dish ran away with the spoon.

1. Duplicate this page for each child.
2. Assist the children in completing the dot-to-dot moon and color if desired.
3. Program the rhyme on a Wolf 1 x 1 grid and use the dot-to-dot moon as the overlay .
4. Send the page home for carryover.

Communication Overlay N - Macaw
Hey Diddle Diddle

Hey Diddle Diddle
The cat & the fiddle

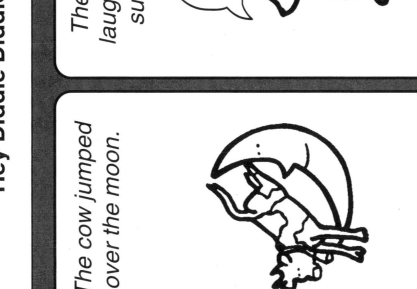

The cow jumped over the moon.

The little dog laughed to see such sport.

Ha! Ha!

And the dish ran away with the spoon.

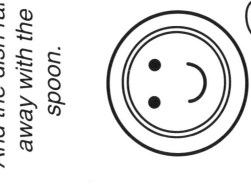

Salt Dough
Recipe Strips

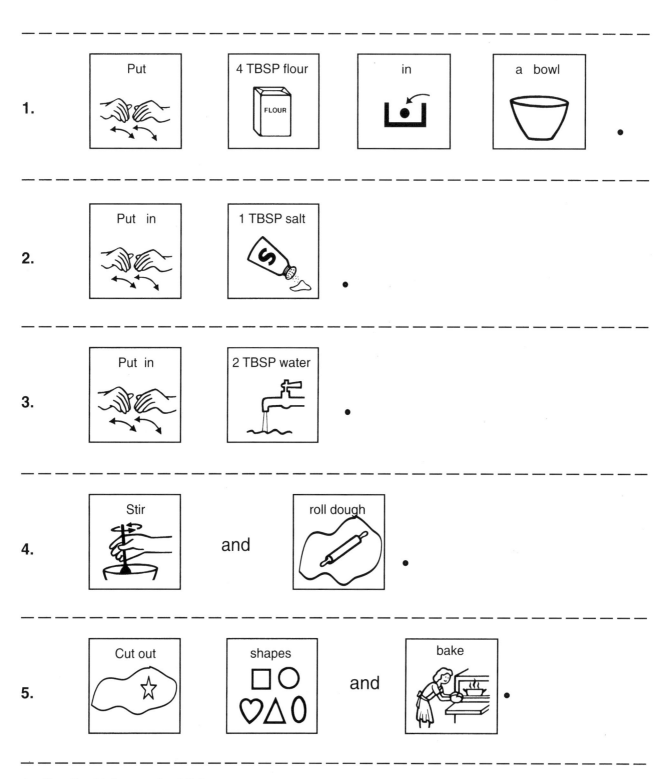

1. Put | 4 TBSP flour | in | a bowl .

2. Put in | 1 TBSP salt .

3. Put in | 2 TBSP water .

4. Stir | and | roll dough .

5. Cut out | shapes | and | bake .

1. Duplicate for each child
2. Cut into strips.
3. Let children follow the recipe as they prepare the salt-dough shapes.

Letter Boxes

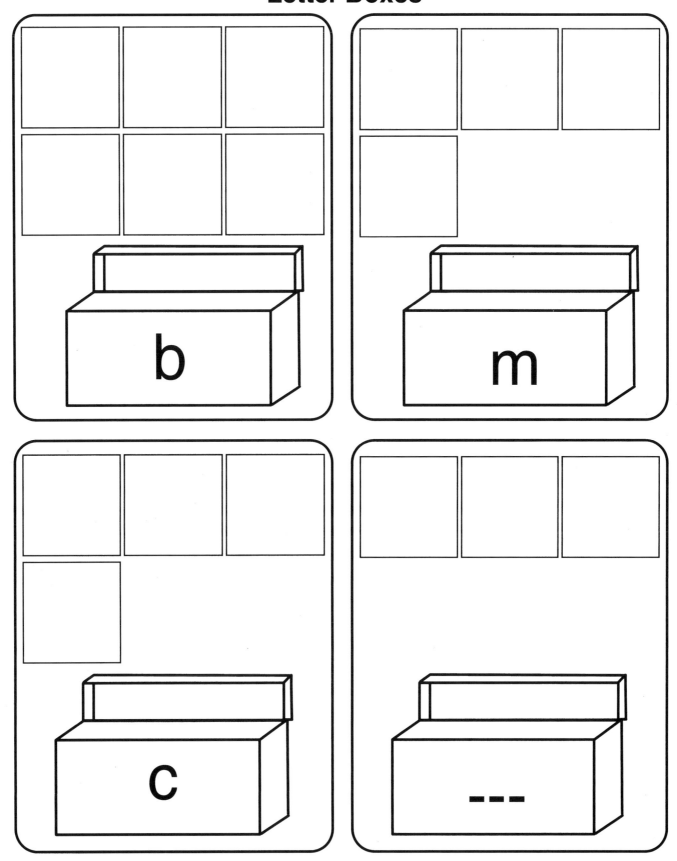

1. Duplicate pages 265 and 266 for each child.
2. Add a beginning sound to the last toy box.
3. Have children glue symbols or draw pictures in the boxes above. Items should have the same beginning sound as on the toy box.

Letter Boxes

1. Help "bunny" sort the things in his bedroom by beginning sounds.
2. Cut out the symbols on this page and glue above the correct beginning letter box on the previous page.

Match Up

Match the rhyming word pairs.

bear

chair

kitten

mouse

clock

mush

house

mittens

brush

socks

Seasons of the Year Unit

Seasons Unit

Introduction

In this unit, we explore special times of the year. In *Chicken Soup With Rice,* we learn the names of the months. We celebrate the season of winter with *The Snowy Day* and *Something Is Going to Happen.* We plant a springtime garden in *The Carrot Seed* and eat out with some unusual characters in *The Pigs' Picnic.* The books in this unit are sometimes funny and always fun. The hands-on activities that accompany the stories bring the language to life.

Literature Selections
See page 360 for book sources.
(Note: This unit can be completed using all or a portion of the books listed below.)

Chicken Soup With Rice. Maurice Sendak. Harper and Row., New York.
ISBN: 0-590717-89-8

The Snowy Day. Ezra Jack Keats. The Viking Press., New York.
ISBN: 0-590-73323-0

Something Is Going to Happen. Charlotte Zolotow. Harper and Row., New York.
ISBN: 06-0270-28-4

The Carrot Seed. Ruth Krauss. Harper and Row., New York.
ISBN: 0-064432-10-6

The Pigs' Picnic. Keiko Kasza. G.P. Putnam's Sons., New York.
ISBN: 0-399215-43-3

Seasons Unit
I.E.P. Goals and Objectives

The child will:

- ❏ identify and express:
    - ❏ months.
    - ❏ seasons.
    - ❏ food.
    - ❏ kitchen tools and utensils.
    - ❏ gardening tools and supplies.

- ❏ identify and express the following descriptive concepts:
    - ❏ hot / cold.
    - ❏ colors.
    - ❏ basic adjective concepts.
    - ❏ same / different / matching.

- ❏ identify and express the spatial concepts of:
    - ❏ in.
    - ❏ on.

- ❏ demonstrate the ability to sequence a 3-5 step task.

- ❏ respond to "wh" and "yes / no" questions.

- ❏ respond to content-related questions pertaining to a literature selection.

- ❏ follow and/or give one and two step oral commands.

- ❏ demonstrate basic cooking skills by:
    - ❏ following a simple recipe.
    - ❏ locating appropriate ingredients.
    - ❏ locating kitchen tools.

- ❏ increase pragmatic communication skills by expressing:
    - ❏ negation / rejection.
    - ❏ requests, wants and needs.
    - ❏ approval.
    - ❏ recurrence (more).
    - ❏ preference.
    verbally or using an appropriate augmented communication system.

- ❏ use a switch to initiate an action or recurrence of an action.

- ❏ read and express 3-5 word sentences using PCS.

- ❏ attend to and actively participate in storytime activities.

Seasons - Related Literature

Bear All Year	Harriet Ziefert
Caps, Hats, Socks, and Mittens	Louise Borden
Everything Grows	Raffi
The Jacket I Wear in the Snow	Shirley Neitzel
Out and About	Shirley Hughes
Seasons	Heidi Gonnel
Spring	Louis Santrey
Warm in Winter	Erica Silverman
Winter	Richard Allington

Seasons - Music Resources

"Growing"

Learning Basic Skills Through Music:Vol. 1
Hap Palmer 1969
Educational Activities Inc.
Box 392
Freeport, NY 11520

Raffi

"Everything Grows"

"Months of the Year"

We All Live Together: Vol. 2
Greg & Steve
Little House Music (ASCAP)
Youngheart Records 1978
Los Angeles, CA 90027

"Days of the Week"

We All Live Together: Vol. 4
Greg & Steve
Little House Music (ASCAP)
Youngheart Records 1980
Los Angeles, CA 90027

"The Four Seasons"
"The Magic Seed"

Seasonal Songs
Sing and Learn 1989
Macmillan Book Clubs, Inc.
Macmillan Educational Co.

"Weekday Rock"

Language Skills
Sing and Learn 1989
Macmillan Book Clubs, Inc.
Macmillan Educational Co.

"Apples and Banana"

One Light, One Sun
Raffi
Trabadour Records
Universal City, CA

"Going on a Picnic"

The Corner Grocery Store
Raffi
Trabadour Records
Universal City, CA

Seasons - Computer Resources

Sammy's Science House - Edmark   Seasons, weather
MAC, IBM

Chicken Soup With Rice

by
Maurice Sendak

Summary

What time of year is best for eating chicken soup with rice? That question is answered in this delightful book of months. Maurice Sendak's rhyming text and enchanting pictures take us around the world and through the seasons in a tribute to that most wonderful of foods. Each page features the repeated line "chicken soup with rice," and both the text and illustrations are full of charm and humor. This selection is also available in Big Book format. This is an ideal book for teaching months of the year.

Suggested Activities

Sharing the Story

Read the story out loud using one of the communication overlays on pages 280-281. If you have access to either a felt board or a story board with Velcro® (this is described in the introduction section, page 12), then also duplicate the calendar cards on pages 284-285. Cut out the calendar cards, color, and laminate if desired. Then add a small square of self-stick Velcro® to the back. As you read each page, a child can pick out the appropriate calendar card and place it on the story board. The pictures on the calendar cards parallel the illustrations in the book, so finding each month's card can be a fun activity in itself.

If you have a switch user in your story group, try programming the names of the 12 months on a WOLF using the "list" command. Each time the child pushes his/her switch, the WOLF will speak the name of a month, one for each switch activation, in sequential order. This is an ideal way for a switch user to take an active and important part in reading the story. Programming instructions for the "list" command can be found in the Introduction section of this book on page 15.
NOTE: When reading this story, it may be desirable to change the last line for every page to "Yummy once, yummy twice, yummy chicken soup with rice."

Yuckies and Yummies

This activity can be done individually or as a class project. Duplicate pages 291 and 292 for each child. Identify the picture symbols on page 292 and color if desired. Each child should choose 3 "yummies" and 3 "yuckies" and cut these out. As you glue these onto page 291, read the sentences together. Each child can have a chance to share his/her likes and dislikes with the class.

Chicken Soup with Rice
Assemble the following ingredients:

    6 cups water per child plus 3 chicken bouillon cubes
      (canned chicken broth may be substituted)
    1/2 cup raw rice per each 6 children
    chopped carrots
    chopped celery
    cooked chicken pieces
    salt and pepper to taste

Put the prepared chicken broth or bouillon in a large cooking pot. Chop the carrots, celery, and chicken and add to the soup. Add the raw rice and bring to a boil. Cover the pot and simmer for 15 minutes or until rice is done. Add salt and pepper to taste. Enjoy! If desired, copy the symbol recipe on page 286-287, and cut into strips. Read each sentence and find the ingredients in sequence. Communication overlays for this activity are found on pages 288-289. This recipe serves approximately six children; double if desired.
Variation: Simply serve canned chicken soup with rice.

Silly Soup
Take a large bowl or soup pot and fill to near the top with raw rice. (Dried beans also work well, but watch out for beans in noses and mouths!) Bury various small items under the rice, such as spoons, comb, toothbrush, toy figures, plastic egg, plastic vegetables,etc. Let each child in turn find a buried treasure in the rice. This is a good opportunity to elicit sentences ("I found___") or simply practice noun identification. As the objects are discovered, place them in a pile in the center of the table. As all are found, another game can be made. Can you remember who found what?

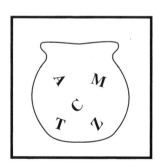

Alphabet Soup
Using the template on page 290, cut out a soup pot form for each child from black construction paper. Glue the soup pots onto a piece of lighter colored construction paper for contrast. Give each child a dish of alphabet cereal. Place several glue dots on the black soup pot, and let the children then glue their cereal pieces onto the dots. To make the soup pot look more "soupy," you can glue on dried beans and rice as well.

This art activity lends itself well to various academic objectives. If a child is learning letter or name recognition skills, you might choose only to put the first letter in his/her name in a letter dish. Other children might practice gluing on the letters in their complete names or other words from a model. Just be careful, or all your art supplies for this activity will soon be gobbled up!

Calendar Lotto/Holiday Lotto

Duplicate one calendar lotto game board for each child (see page 293). For durability, It is suggested that you glue each game board onto card-weight or construction paper, and laminate. The next step is to cut out the calendar lotto cards on page 294. Again, if you would like to keep them permanently, glue each card onto a square of heavy paper, and laminate.

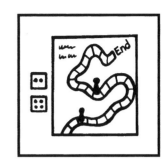

Calendar lotto is a matching game. Put the game pieces face down on the table. Each child chooses a piece in turn, and covers the appropriate square on his/her game board. If a child chooses a piece he does not need, play passes to the next player. The winner is the first to completely cover a game board.

If you have a child in your group who does not yet have matching skills, try pairing him/her with another player. One child can have the assignment of picking the cards; the other child places them on the game board. It's also fun to "jazz up" the game by throwing in a few wild cards. Kids love lotto games so have some fun!

Variation: Holiday lotto is a slightly more difficult game—the players must match a holiday to the month in which it occurs.

Carryover Activities

Pages 296-297

Chicken soup with rice!

Communication Overlay B - Macaw

Yummy!

Chicken soup with rice!

Communication Overlay C - Wolf

January		July	
February		August	
March		September	
April		October	
May		November	
June		December	

Communication Overlay D - Macaw

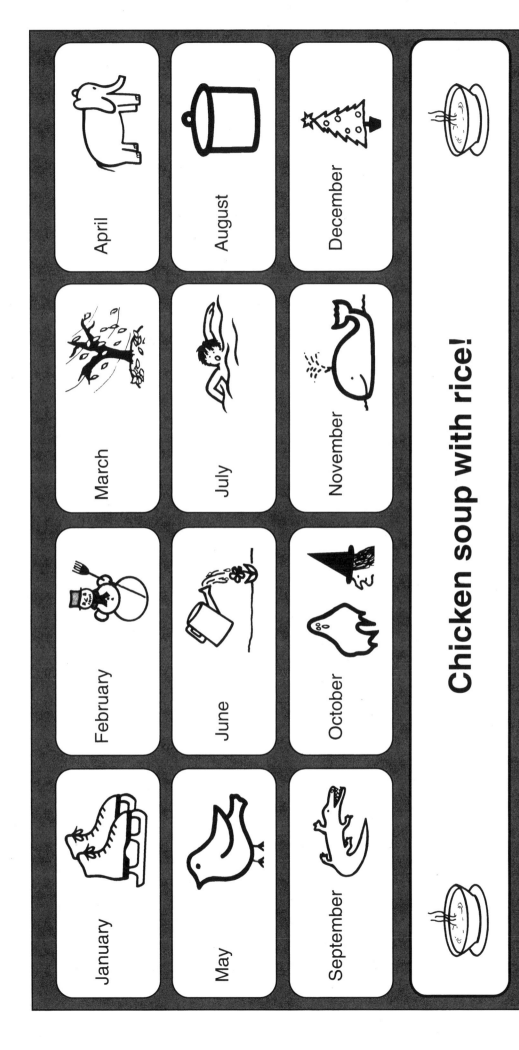

Chicken soup with rice!

Chicken Soup With Rice
Calendar Cards

January	February
March	April
May	June

Chicken Soup With Rice
Calendar Cards

Chicken Soup With Rice
Recipe Strips

1.

Put	broth	in	pot
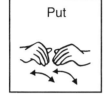		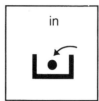	

.

2.

Cut	carrots
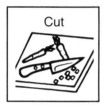	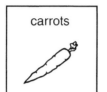

.

3.

Put	carrots	in	pot
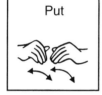	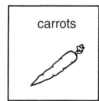	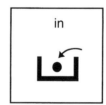	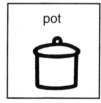

.

4.

Cut	celery
	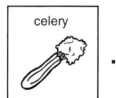

.

5.

Put	celery	in	pot
	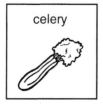	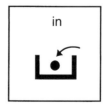	

.

6. Cut chicken .

7. Put chicken in pot .

8. Put rice in pot .

9. Put pot on stove .

Communication Overlay E - Wolf

cut

put in

stir

carrots

celery

chicken

rice

soup

my turn

Communication Overlay F - Macaw

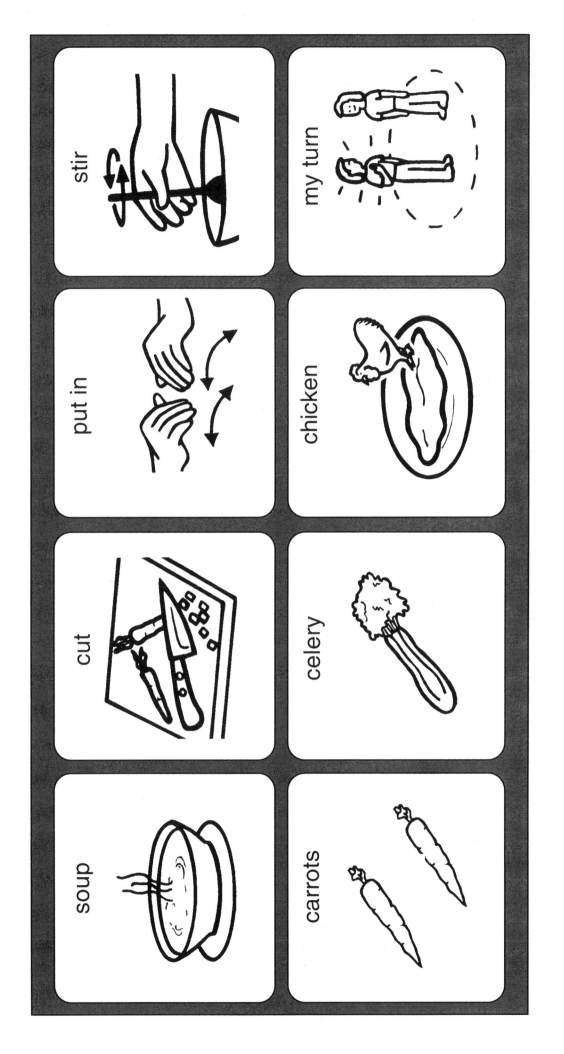

Using black construction paper, cut out one soup pot form for each child.

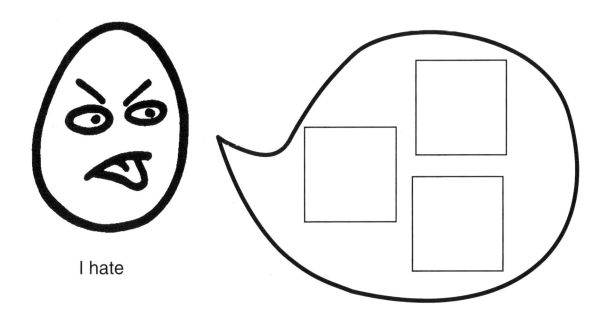

I hate

- -

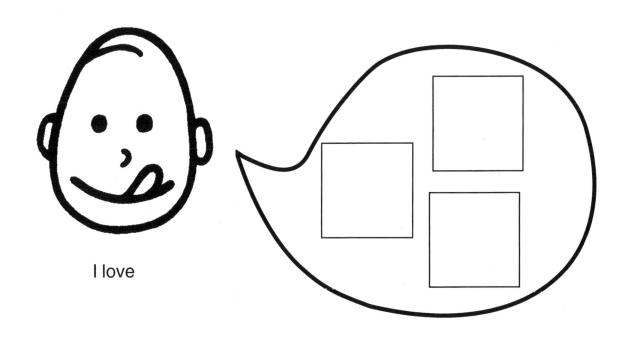

I love

name

Yuckies and Yummies

ice cream

pickles

chips

salad

french fries

pizza

onions

popcorn

taco

broccoli

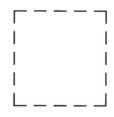

Draw your own!

1. Identify food items. Color if desired.
2. Find 3 "yuckies" and 3 "yummies" and cut out.
3. Glue the picture symbols onto the worksheet page and read the sentences together.

Calendar and Holiday Lotto
Game Board

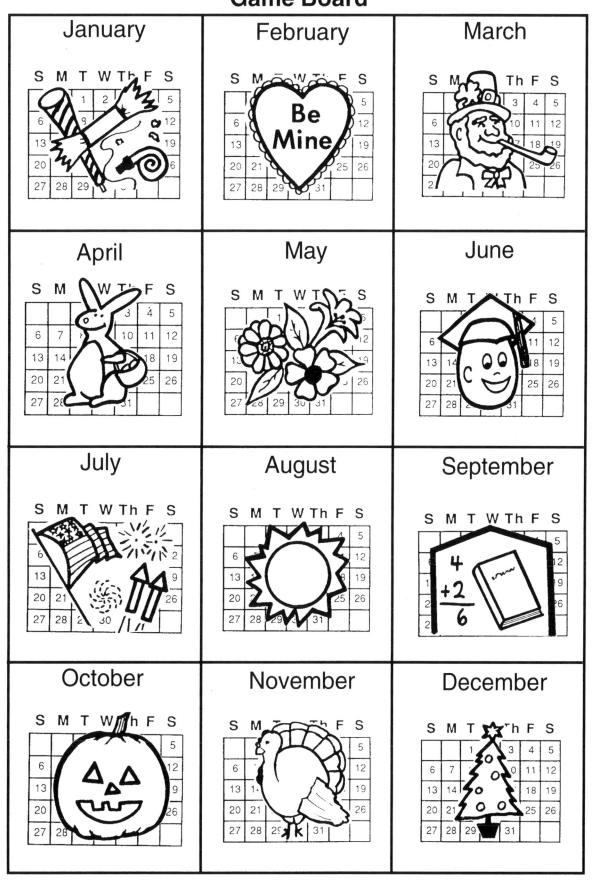

Chicken Soup With Rice
Calendar Lotto Cards

1. Duplicate this page twice (or more for more players).
2. Cut out each card and glue onto squares of card-weight or construction paper.
3. Laminate if desired.

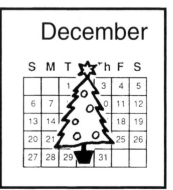

Chicken Soup With Rice
Holiday Lotto Cards

1. Duplicate this page twice (or more for more players).
2. Cut out each card and glue onto squares of card-weight or construction paper.
3. Laminate if desired.

New Year's Day	Valentine's Day	St. Pat's Day

Easter	Mother's Day	Father's Day

Fourth of July	August	September
		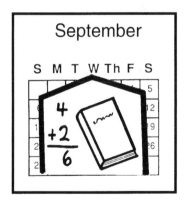

Halloween	Thanksgiving	Christmas

Chicken Soup With Rice
What goes in the soup?

Directions: Color the appropriate items. Read the symbol sentence together.

rice

apple

celery

carrot

chicken

bread

onions

peanut butter

I

put

in

soup

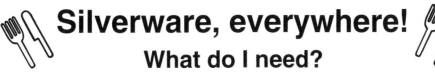 # Silverware, everywhere!

What do I need?

spoon

ice cream

cake

fork

applesauce

soup

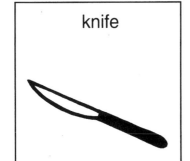

knife

pie

meat

Directions: Draw a line to the food item(s) eaten with each utensil shown below.

The Snowy Day
by
Ezra Jack Keats

Summary

Peter wakes up one morning and looks out his window. Snow covers the city as far as he can see. He spends a day outdoors in the snow--making footprints and snow angels, a snowman, and sliding down snowdrift mountains. He ends the day in a warm bath, thinking about his adventures. This book is a Caldecott Medal winner. The storyline is whimsical and simple, and the illustrations enchanting. This is a great book to share when a snowfall is eminent.

Suggested Activities

Sharing the Story

Read the story using the communication overlays on pages 302-303. A pair of shoes and a stick are useful props for the section of the story where Peter makes footprints, as well as a bright red jacket or snowsuit to mirror the one Peter wears. Let the children act out making the "inny" and "outy" footprints with Peter. By all means, make snow angels if you live in a part of the country where you can do so. (Here in Georgia we just make them on the floor!)

Snowy Songs

The classic snowy day song is, of course, "Jingle Bells." This has been recorded by various artists, including Raffi, but is equally fun when sung alone. Try to obtain a chiming bells switch toy to include switch users in the fun. You can also get bells to shake from music teachers, or better yet, read on to make your own.

Jingle Bells

Distribute two aluminum pie pans to each child--the disposable kind sold in grocery stores. Have a bowl of dried beans on the table (black-eyed peas, pinto beans, etc.), and let each child put a handful into his or her pie plate. Put the other plate on top, and staple around the edges. Decorations can be as simple as Christmas stickers, or holes can be punched around the edges and laced with colored yarn. Instant music!
Variation: Use paper plates and decorate with stickers or markers.

Snowy Trees

Collect a large pine cone for each child. If your school has a place nearby where you can walk and let children find their own, even better! Stand the pine cones upright on a newspaper-covered table, and let each child paint the outside of the cone with white paint. (The paint does not need to completely cover the inside part of the pine cone). While still wet, sprinkle with silver glitter for a beautiful winter tree sparkling with snow.

If desired, miniature clay plant pots (available at nursery and variety stores) make attractive stands for the pine cone trees. Simply apply a thick ring of glue around the rim of the pot, and place the pine cone on top. A bright red ribbon encircling the pot completes the display.

Popcorn Snowmen

Help Peter make a snowman! Melt 1/4 c. butter and one 10 oz. package of marshmallows in an electric or regular skillet.Stir frequently. When melted, remove from heat and stir in approximately 6 cups of popped popcorn. This will make a stiff yet still shapeable mixture. Butter the children's hands to prevent sticking. Give each child a handful of the warm popcorn mix. Shape the mix into a ball and place on buttered wax paper. Repeat this process with a smaller amount of mixture to make a smaller ball to place on top of the first. Repeat again for a 3-ball snowman, if desired. Add facial features using candy pieces or raisins.

NOTE: Expand this activity by making popcorn. Directions for preparing popcorn are provided on overlays found on pages 304 and 305. Be prepared to double the recipe for a larger group, or make two batches.

Frosty Footprints

Using refrigerated, canned biscuit dough, pass out one biscuit round to each child. In addition, give each child five small pieces of biscuits to be shaped into balls. These are pressed onto the top edge of the large biscuit to form toes. The artistically minded can elongate the larger biscuit round to look more like a foot. Bake according to package directions. After cooling for five minutes, give a snowy topping to each footprint by spreading white frosting or butter on top. (Total number of biscuits required--2 per child.)

Peter's Winter Window

These worksheets create a charming make-and-take reading activity for school and home. Duplicate pages 306 and 307 for each child. Color if desired (especially Peter's window curtains and the symbols on the picture wheel). Cut out the window opening where indicated, and cut out the picture wheel. Using a two-pronged metal fastener, fasten the picture wheel behind the window opening. (The black dot indicates where to position the fastener.) Turning the picture wheel creates five different scenes from Peter's window. As the wheel is turned, read the symbol sentence to describe the view.

Dress Peter for a Snowy Day

Duplicate pages 308 and 309 for each child. Color and cut out the clothing pictures. (In the story, Peter's snowsuit is a beautiful bright red). Using gluesticks, "dress" Peter for his snowy day. Read the symbol sentences as you go.

Carryover Activities

Pages 310-312

Communication Overlay A - Wolf

It's snowing!

coat, snowsuit

footprints

tree

snowman

snow angel

mother

Peter took a bath.

Let's go play!

302

Communication Overlay B - Macaw

snowman

Let's go play!

footprints

Peter took a bath.

coat, snowsuit

mother

It's snowing!

snow angel

Communication Overlay C - Wolf

We need a bowl.

Put in the popcorn.

Turn on the popcorn popper.

I want some popcorn!

304

Communication Overlay D - Macaw

| We need a bowl. | Put in the popcorn. | Turn on the popcorn popper. | I want some popcorn! |

Snowy Winter Window

Peter looked out his window.

What did he see?

cut out shaded area

Peter

saw

_____ .

Peter's Winter Window

Picture Wheel

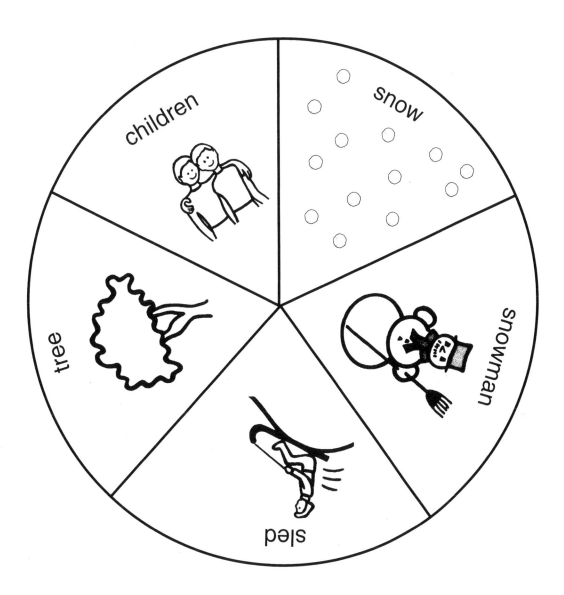

1. Color worksheet pages if desired.

2. Cut out window opening where indicated. Cut out picture wheel.

3. Using a two-prong metal fastener, fasten the picture wheel behind the window opening so that pictures are viewed through the window.

4. Turn the wheel as you read the symbol sentences.

The Snowy Day
Dress Peter for a snowy day!

Put   snowsuit   hat   boots   mittens   on   Peter

The Snowy Day
Dress Peter for a snowy day!

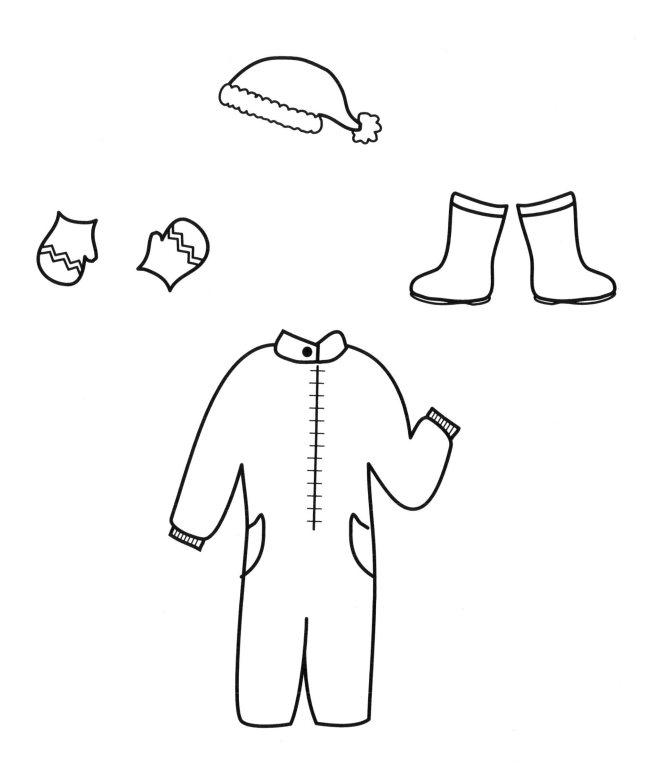

The Snowy Day

Who made the footprints?

Instructions: Draw lines from each footprint to "who" made it.

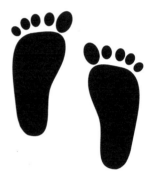

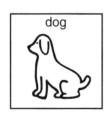

Match and color the big and little snowmen.

The Snowy Day
Tell Me About It!

1. What did Peter see out his window?

sun	rain	snow	airplane
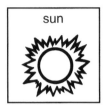			

- -

2. What did Peter wear outside?

sandals	snowsuit	belt	shorts
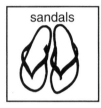		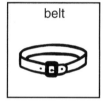	

- -

3. What did Peter make in the snow

snowball	angel	snake	snowman

- -

4. What did Peter do inside his house?

watch T.V.	take a bath	read	listen to music

- -

Instructions:
1. Cut into strips if desired.
2. Children can point to or mark correct answers.

Something Is Going to Happen
by
Charlotte Zolotow

Summary

One by one, the members of a family wake up. One by one, they all have a funny feeling. Something is going to happen. The day starts normally: getting dressed, eating breakfast, gathering books for school. But no one can shake the feeling that this day is somehow different than the one before. When the family opens the door to go outside, the secret is revealed. Something **has** happened. The world is covered with a soft blanket of new snow.

Suggested Activities

Sharing the Story

Read the story using one of the communication overlays on pages 315-317. Take the time to introduce the story characters. Provide toy props for these or photo library pictures to reinforce the vocabulary. This story has a repeated line ("something is going to happen") which can be said together or in turn. One delightful prop to have for the end of the story is an old-fashioned snow globe. Let everyone have a turn shaking it and creating his/her own little snowstorm.

Hot Chocolate

Make everyone's favorite winter-day drink! Using one of the communication overlays on page 318 or 319, make this simple recipe requiring only hot water and instant cocoa mix. As a carryover activity, color, assemble and read the make-and-take sequence book on pages 320 through 322.

Snowball Cookies

Assemble the following ingredients:

> 1 cup butter
> 1/2 cup confectioner's sugar
> 3/4 cup walnuts or pecans (finely chopped)
> 2 1/4 cup flour
> 1 tsp. vanilla

Mix all ingredients. Dust the table and children's hands with flour. Have the children form the dough into 1" balls. Place these on an ungreased cookie sheet and bake for 10 minutes in a 300° oven. Allow to cool, then roll the cookies in confectioner's sugar. This recipe makes approximately 2 dozen cookies.

Popcorn Pictures

If you can manage not to eat it, next time you make popcorn, save a small bowlful to create snowy-day pictures. Provide each child with a piece of blue construction paper for background. Have a precut strip of white paper for each child. Assist the child in gluing this across the bottom edge of the blue paper. This creates snowy white ground against a blue sky. Add other items if desired: houses, trees, etc. Now dot the blue sky with liquid white glue, squeezing random drops of glue on the blue paper. The children then place the popcorn pieces on the glue dots--creating a snowy winter sky.

Pasta Snowflakes

Make a snowflake snowstorm inside your room. Materials include a bag full of wagon-wheel shaped pasta pieces, a pie plate filled with white glue, and a piece on wax paper for each child. For every student, roll one piece of the pasta in the dish of glue (completely around the edges) and place on the piece of wax paper. Place dry pieces of the pasta around the center glued piece, and press lightly so the new pieces will be set firmly in the glue. Add more pieces around the outside by dipping additional pasta wheels in the glue and adding to the snowflake. Allow to dry until set.

When the snowflake is dry, peel it from the wax paper and paint it white (spray paint can be used). Add clear or silver glitter if desired. Hang these from the ceiling using clear plastic line. This creates a glittering snowstorm.

Carryover Activities

Pages 323-325

Communication Overlay A - Wolf

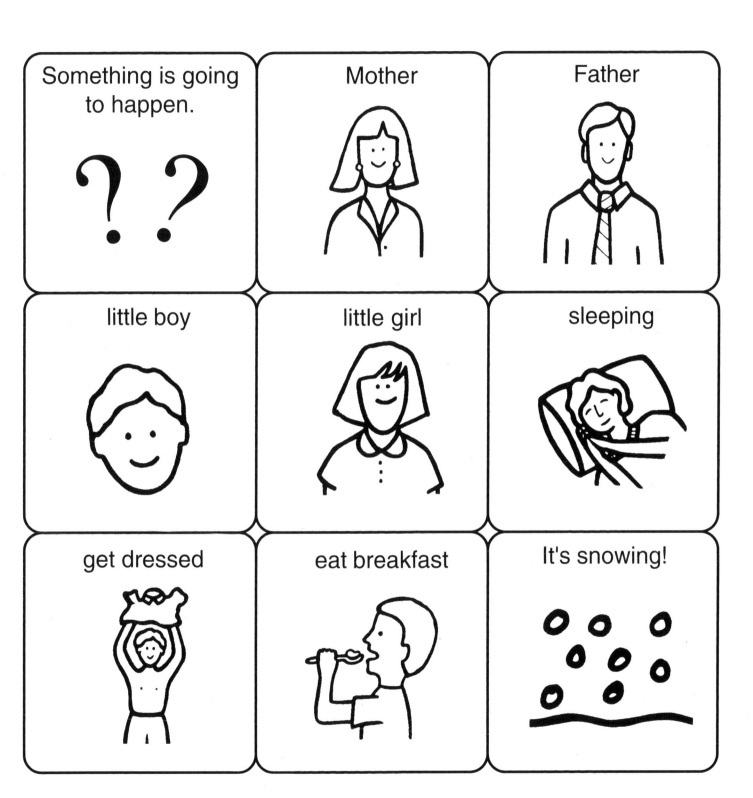

Something is going to happen.

Mother

Father

little boy

little girl

sleeping

get dressed

eat breakfast

It's snowing!

Communication Overlay B - Macaw

Something is going to happen. ???	little girl 
Mother 	sleeping 
Father 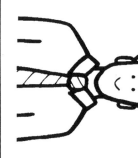	get dressed 
little boy	It's snowing! 

Communication Overlay D - Wolf

I need a cup.

Put in some water.

Put in some chocolate mix.

I need to stir.

Communication Overlay E - Macaw

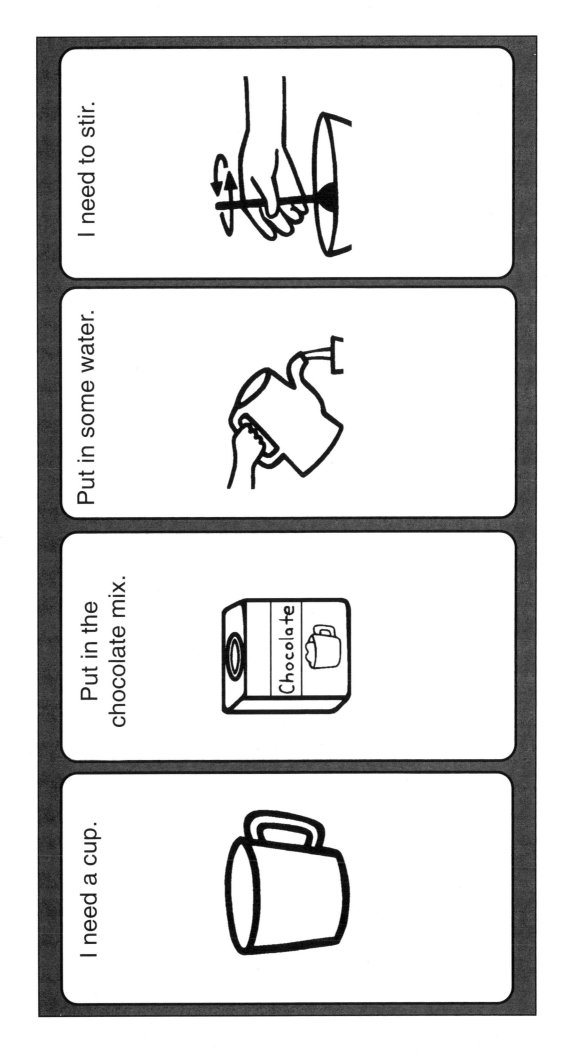

I need to stir.

Put in some water.

Put in the chocolate mix.

I need a cup.

Hot Chocolate
Page 1

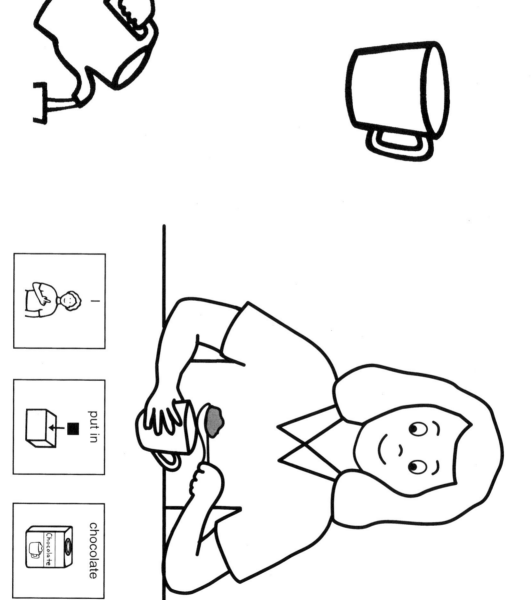

chocolate · put in · —

Hot Chocolate
Page 2

	pour	water
I		the

Hot Chocolate
Page 3

	stir	hot chocolate
I		the

the

hot chocolate

.

Something Is Going to Happen
Tell me about it!

1. What animal lived with the family?

bird	horse	fish	dog
		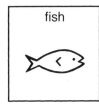	

- -

2. What meal did the mother cook?

pizza	breakfast	snack	dinner

- -

3. What did the family do in the morning?

eat	watch TV	get dressed	read

- -

4. What happened when they went outside?

it rained	it was hot	it snowed

- -

1. Cut out into strips if desired.
2. Children can point to or mark correct answers.

Something is Going to Happen
What happens next?

Using the pictures on the following page, paste the picture in the square that shows what happens next if you see . . .

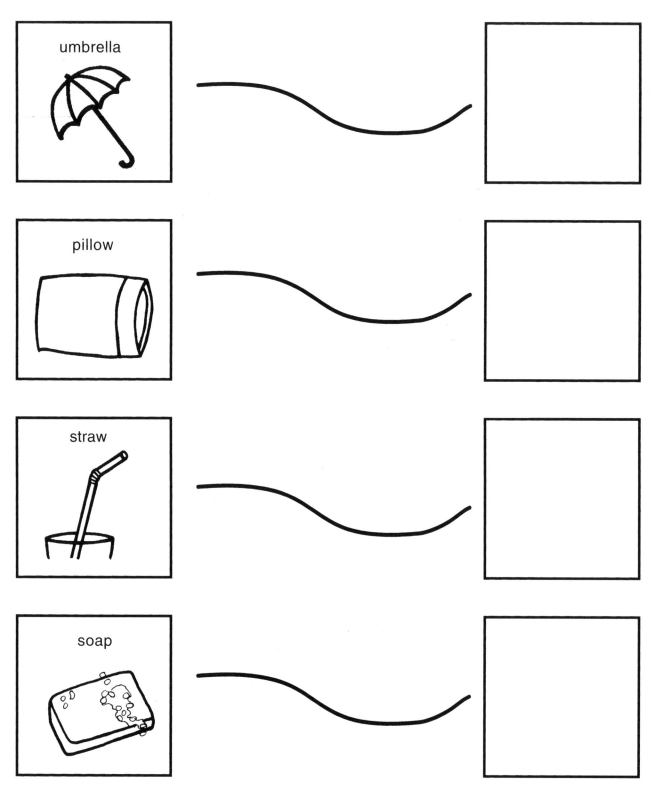

324

Something Is Going to Happen
What happens next?

Color, cut out, and glue these pictures into the appropriate squares on the previous page.

The Carrot Seed
by
Ruth Krauss

Summary

A little boy plants a carrot seed. All his family members tell him, "It won't come up!" But the little boy doesn't give up. Everyday he waters and everyday he weeds. And guess what grows in his garden!

This is a classic children's story, first published in 1945. It is available in Big Book format. It features a repetitive line and a predictable sequence of events. Its charm lies in its language and the clear and charming illustrations. A perfect springtime story.

Suggested Activities

Sharing the Story

Read this story around a table if you are planning to go directly to the seed planting activity. Use communication overlays on pages 329-332. The materials for seed planting make excellent props, along with a real carrot. Have a snack of carrot sticks!

Garden Songs

Assemble food items or pictures as props (peas, corn, carrots, tomatoes, and spinach) and sing "Do you like vegetables?" (See music resources page 274.) Use communication overlays on page 333 or 334. Also try Raffi's recording of "Everything Grows" or "In My Garden."

Planting Seeds

Remember the seed in the little paper cup? All children should do this at least once when growing up!

Assemble materials prior to class: potting soil poured into a tray or large pot; a scooper or small trowel; one paper cup per child; a source of water (a small watering can is great); a packet of seeds. Carrot seeds are obviously desirable, but radish and marigold seeds are foolproof. This is a perfect opportunity to offer a choice.

Copy page 339 to provide plant markers and name tags. Have children choose, cut out, and color a plant marker, and glue to Popsicle sticks. Use overlay on page 335 for requesting materials. Plant according to seed packet directions. Insert a plant marker in each cup. This is a messy activity but well worth it as you watch the seeds sprout in your window.

Mud Pudding
Place plain vanilla or chocolate cookies in a heavy plastic bag. Assist children in rolling the bag with a rolling pin until crumbs are formed.

Using overlay on page 336 or 337, make instant chocolate pudding according to package directions. Use a blender, switch, and environmental control device if possible. Pour the pudding and cookie crumbs into a large bowl and stir until thoroughly mixed. Spoon pudding mixture into paper cups for each child. Insert gummy worms for a yucky, yummy treat!

Carrot Muffins
This recipe works best if a food processor is available (rather than a blender). Couple the food processor with an environmental control unit to provide access for switch users.

Obtain the necessary ingredients to prepare spice cake from a standard cake mix. Make the batter with your class according to package directions. Add cleaned and peeled raw carrots into a food processor equipped with a grater-blade and turn on via switch. Add the grated carrots to the spice cake batter and stir. Cook in muffin tins lined with muffin cups. Bake and enjoy!

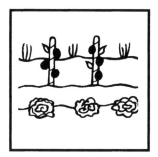

What's growing in the garden?
Copy pages 338-339 for each child. Color and cut out the plant tags and glue onto Popsicle sticks. Color the garden scene (especially the brown dirt), and cut the slits where marked. Glue this sheet around the edges and place on construction-paper backing. As you read each sentence, insert the plant markers into the garden. This makes a great take-home reading activity.

Carryover Activities

Pages 340-343

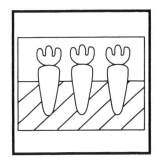

Carrot Patch Art

Use a piece of pop-up sponge (available at craft stores) and cut out two shapes: One for the body of the carrot and the other for the top of the carrot, as shown here.

Mount each of these on a block with a hot glue gun. Once mounted, moisten the sponges until they "Pop up," ready to be used for sponge printing. **NOTE: Don't moisten the sponge until glue attaching the sponge to the block is set.**

Each child will need one large piece of blue construction paper (12 x 18 inches) and, a large piece of brown construction paper cut along its length to a rectangle of 8 x 18 inches. In addition, two paper plates will be needed to hold the paint. Help the children squeeze orange and green paint onto the paper plates—these will be used for the sponge painting.

Next, each child squeezes glue onto the brown paper, and pats it down onto the blue sheet—even along the bottom. This forms the garden (dirt beneath a blue sky). Dip the carrot pop-up sponge into the orange paint, and stamp carrots onto the brown dirt. Once done, dip the carrot top pop-up sponge into the green paint, and stamp the tops onto the carrots.

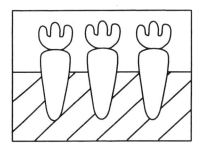

Have fun counting the carrots in your patch! For the scientifically minded, this is a good time to talk about how carrots grow down into the dirt.

329

Communication Overlay A - Wolf

No! It won't come up.

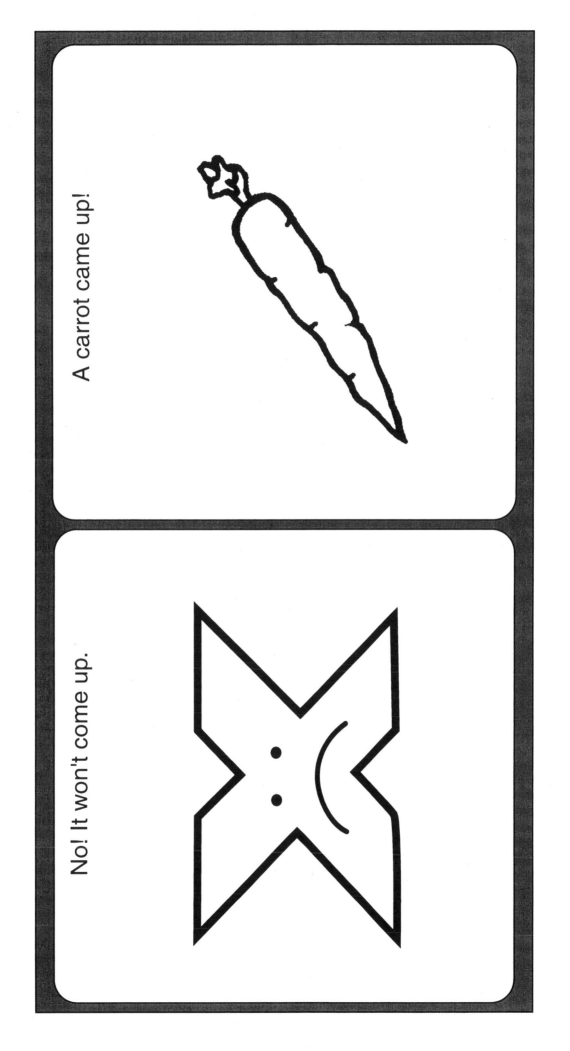

Communication Overlay B - Macaw

No! It won't come up.

A carrot came up!

Communication Overlay C - Wolf

carrot seeds	No! It won't come up!	mother
father	big brother	Nothing came up!
Water the plants.	Pull the weeds.	A carrot came up!

Communication Overlay D - Macaw

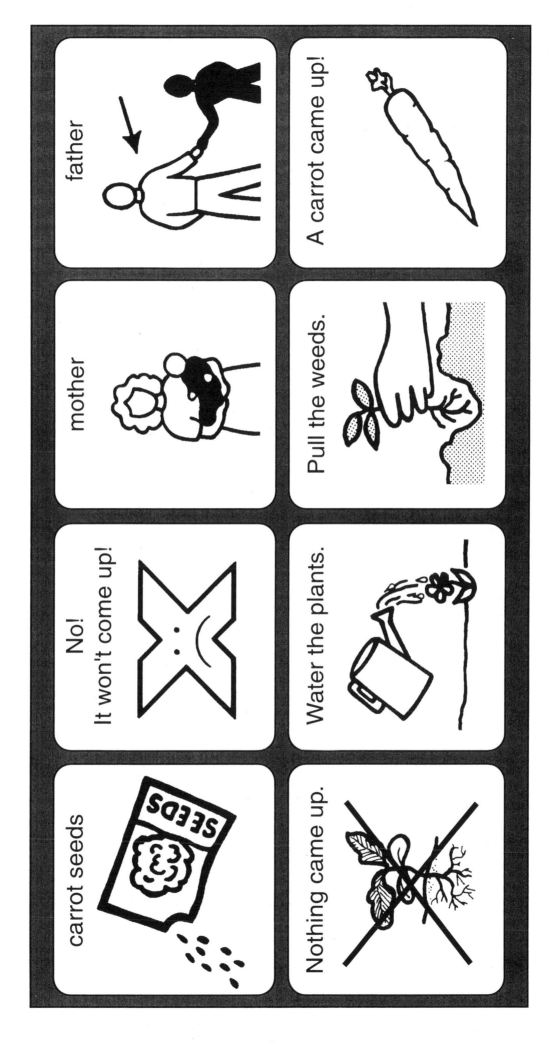

father

mother

No!
It won't come up!

carrot seeds

A carrot came up!

Pull the weeds.

Water the plants.

Nothing came up.

Communication Overlay E - Wolf

Do you like?	vegetables	peas
corn	carrots	tomatoes
spinach		Yes, I do!

NOTE: Program in another
vegetable if desired.

Communication Overlay F - Macaw

Communication Overlay G - Wolf

I need a cup.

Now I need some dirt.

Put the seeds in.

Put on some water!

SEEDS

Communication Overlay H - Wolf

cookies	rolling pin	pudding mix
milk	Turn on the blender.	bowl
spoon	Put in some gummy worms.	Let's eat!

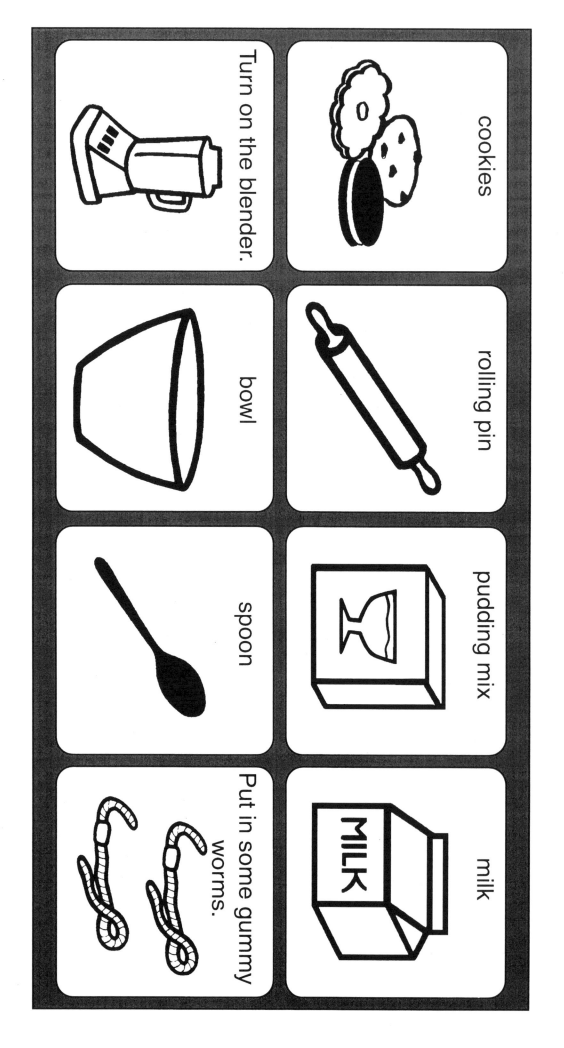

Communication Overlay I - Macaw

cookies

Turn on the blender.

rolling pin

bowl

pudding mix

spoon

milk

Put in some gummy worms.

What's growing in the garden?

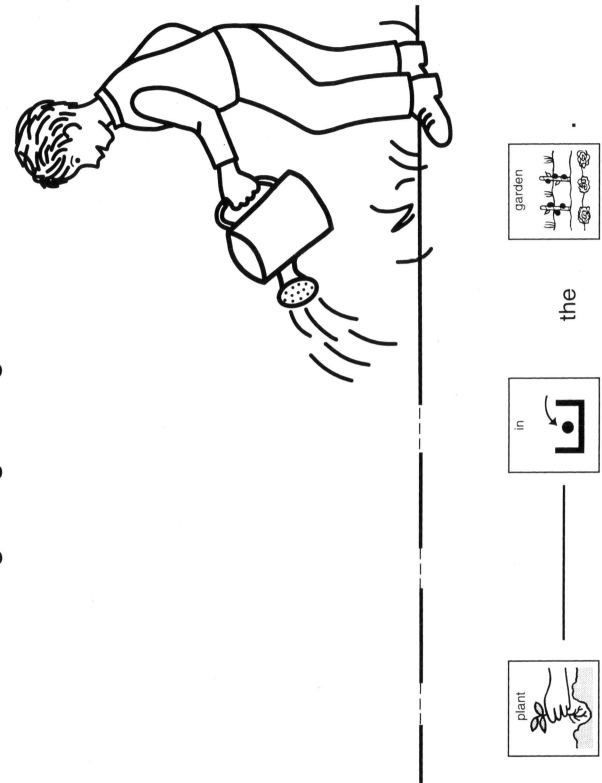

plant _____ in the garden.

Cut slits on dotted lines.

What's growing in the garden?

carrot

potato

broccoli

corn

1. Color plant tags, then cut out along dotted lines.

2. Glue each plant tag on a popsicle stick.

3. Place each tag into a slot cut on the "What's growing in the garden?" worksheet as you read the symbol sentences.

The Carrot Seed
Tell Me About It!

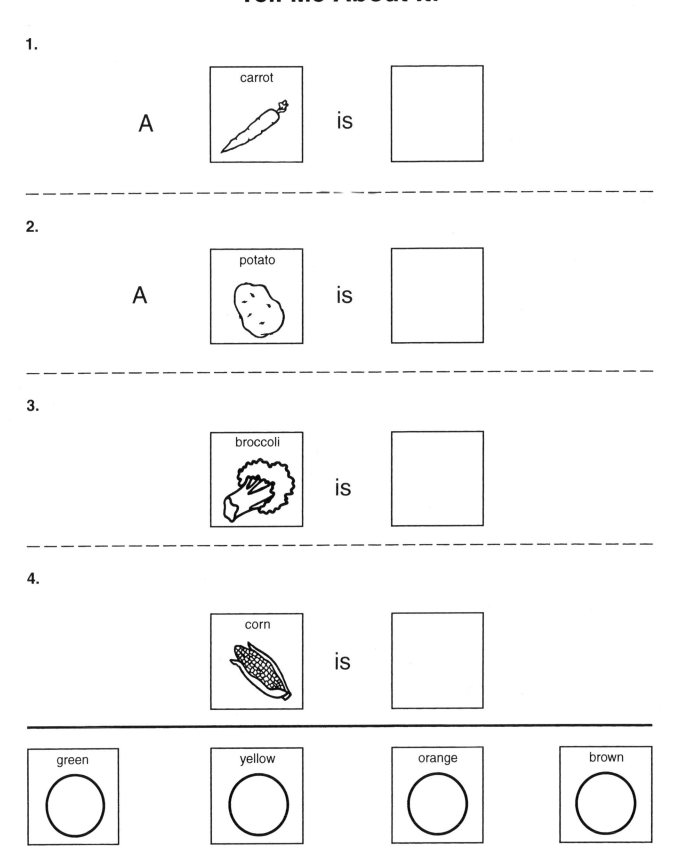

1.

A   carrot   is

2.

A   potato   is

3.

broccoli   is

4.

corn   is

green   yellow   orange   brown

Color in each circle. Cut circles out and glue in the appropriate space above.

341

Tell Me About It!

1. Color and cut out the symbols on the bottom of each page.

2. Glue each symbol in the appropriate box as the symbol sentence is read.

The Carrot Seed
Find and Color the Vegetables

carrot

orange

apple

banana

potato

broccoli

peas

How many carrots?

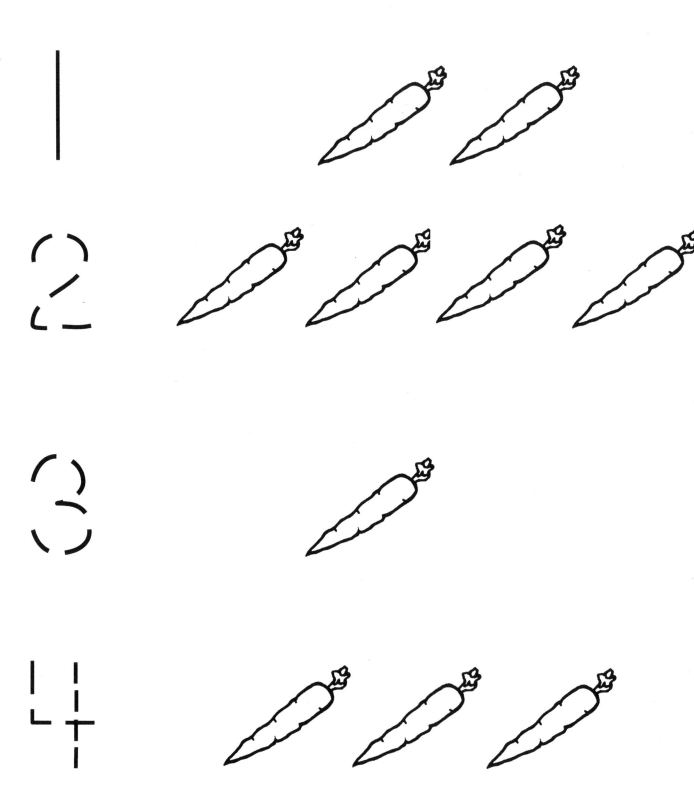

Match the number with the correct group of carrots.

The Pigs' Picnic
by
Keiko Kasza

Summary

On a beautiful spring day, Mr. Pig decides to invite his friend Miss Pig out for a picnic. On his way, he meets his friends, who convince him to borrow some of their finery in order to make a good impression. He borrows a tail from the fox, some magnificent hair from the lion, and some racy stripes from the zebra. The result, to say the least, is quite alarming. Miss Pig screams when she sees him, and Mr. Pig runs away, returning all that he has borrowed. He goes back to Miss Pig's house, who is quite relieved to see him after such a terrifying visit from an unknown monster. A quiet picnic with her good friend sounds like just the thing.

Suggested Activities

Sharing the Story

Read the story, using one of the communication overlays on page 347 or 348. Have available props necessary to dress Mr. Pig for his picnic: a tail (a piece of rope or a strip of fake fur make good substitutes), the lion's hair (an old wig), and stripes from the zebra (a striped T-shirt will do, or a long strip of material that can be wrapped around a child). Have each student take a turn being Mr. Pig. Other students can offer their finery at the appropriate parts of the story and have fun dressing up their classmate in his alarming outfit.

Fun with Music

After reading the story, try learning this song. Assemble the following props: a picnic basket and various play foods to go inside (fruits, sandwiches, dessert items, and drinks are all good choices). Put the basket on the floor, and the food items on a colorful cloth beside it. To the tune of "John Brown's Body" / "Glory, Glory Hallelujah" sing:

> I am going on a picnic,
> I am going on a picnic,
> I am going on a picnic,
> I think I'll bring some _____!

Let each child choose and name an item for the picnic, and add it to the basket during the last line of the song. Try adding some silly things too. Do you really want to pack that old shoe to eat?

Lunchmeat Sandwiches
Make some sandwiches to enjoy for an outdoor meal. Duplicate the recipe strips found on pages 351-352 and cut along the dotted lines. Read the symbol sentences together as you assemble the sandwiches. The recipe strips can be put in the correct order and bound along the left edge with staples to create a take-home reading activity. Overlays for AAC users are included on pages 349 and 350. When the sandwiches are ready, pack them into a picnic basket, take outside, and enjoy!

Packing a Picnic
As a classroom activity, plan and pack an outdoor lunch. Making lunchmeat sandwiches can serve as the main course. What else goes into a picnic lunch?

As a carryover activity, photocopy the picnic lunch pages 353 and 354 for each child. As you paste the picnic items on the table cloth, read the symbol sentences together.

What will Mr. Pig wear?
Dress up Mr. Pig in his picnic finery. Duplicate page 356 for each child. With a crayon, color Mr. Pig pink. Now add his striking (but odd) picnic outfit. With a black crayon, add stripes. Hair can be added with crayon or by drizzling glue on the top of his head. To the glue, stick some cut up bits of yarn, or sprinkle on some glitter. The tail can also be added with crayon or yarn and glue. Take some time to talk about Mr. Pig's new clothes. How does he look?
What could he wear instead?

Carryover Activities

Pages 357-358

Communication Overlay A - Wolf

Mr. Pig	picnic	It's a monster!
fox	lion	zebra
tail	hair	stripes

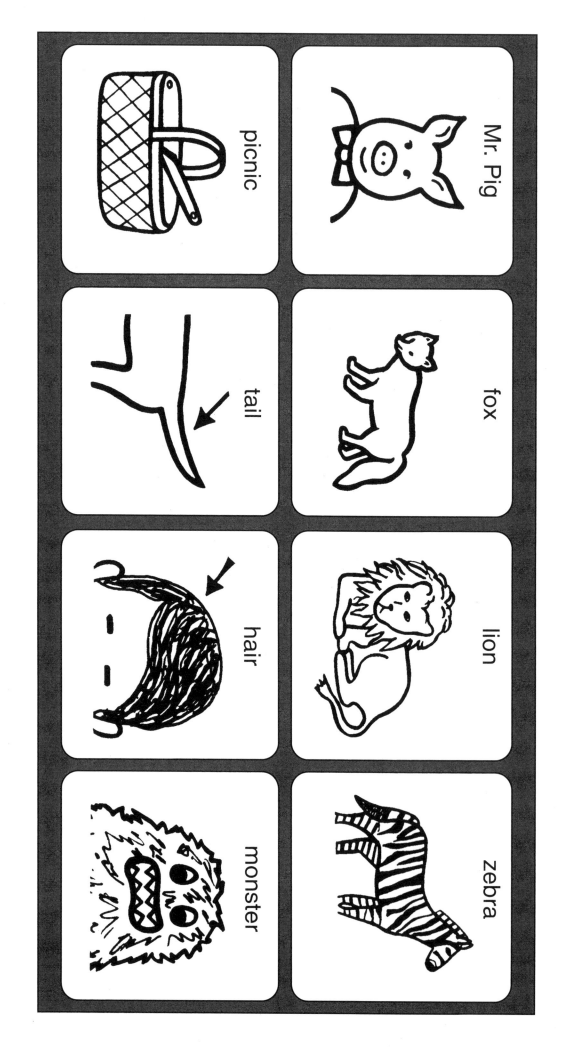

Communication Overlay B - Macaw

Communication Overlay C - Wolf

open	put on	spread
bread	lunch meat	cheese
mustard/mayonnaise	knife	sandwich

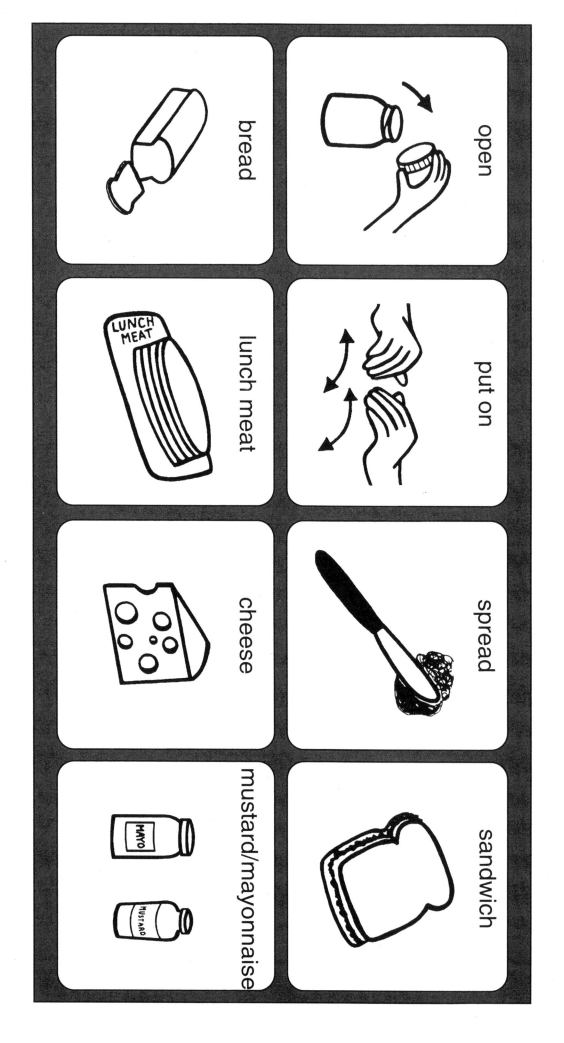

Communication Overlay D - Macaw

The Pigs' Picnic
Recipe Strips

1.
Open
bread
.

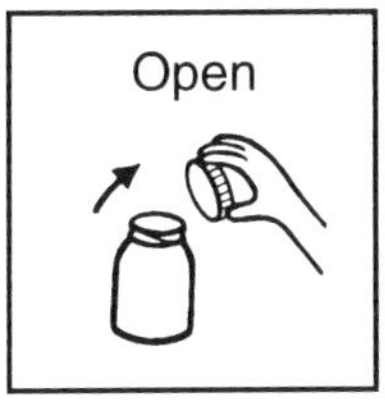

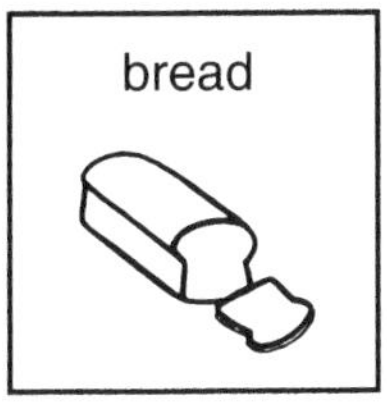

2.
Get
2
bread slices
.

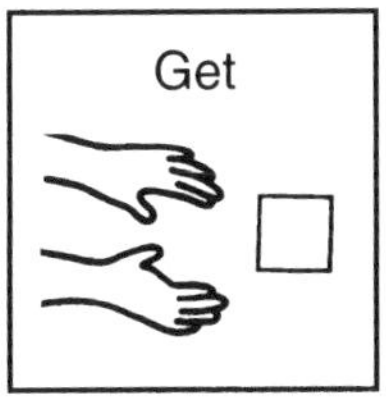

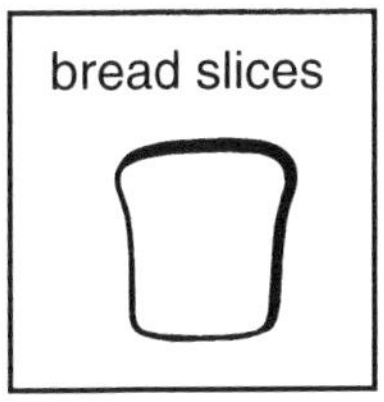

3.
Open
mayonnaise/
mustard
MAYO
.

4.
Spread
mayonaise/
mustard
MAYO
.

5.
Put on
lunch meat
LUNCH MEAT
.

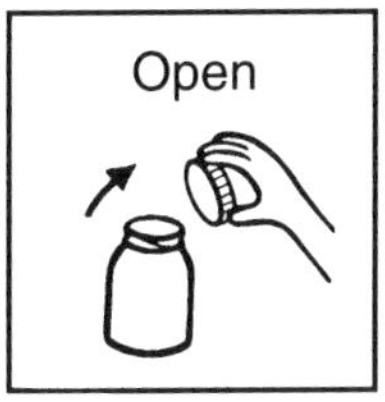

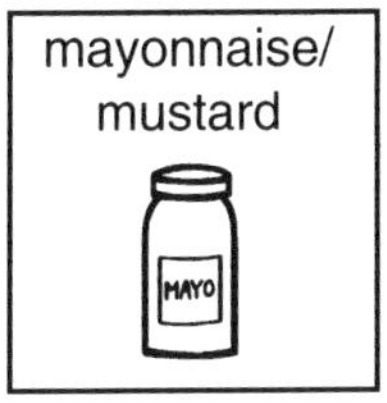

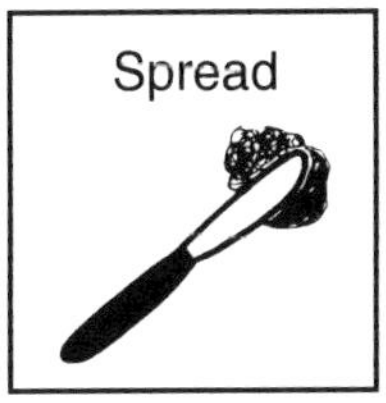

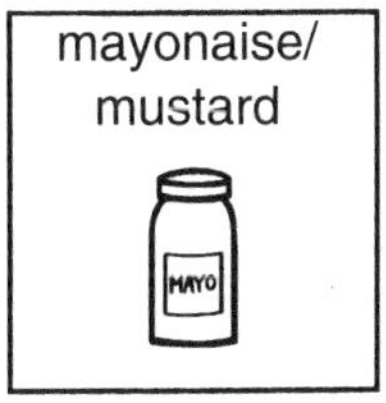

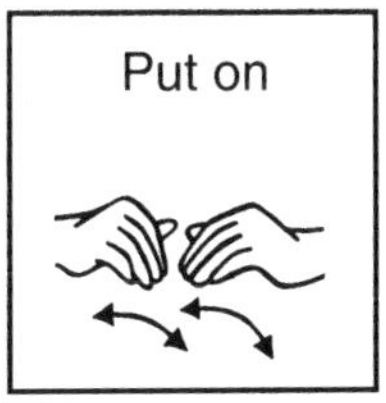

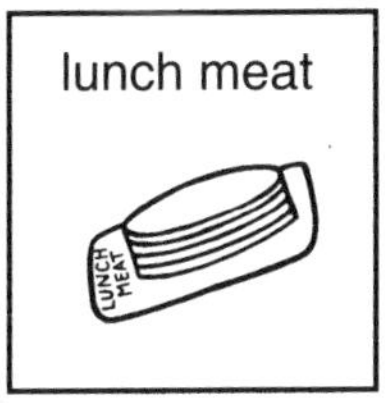

The Pigs' Picnic
Recipe Strips

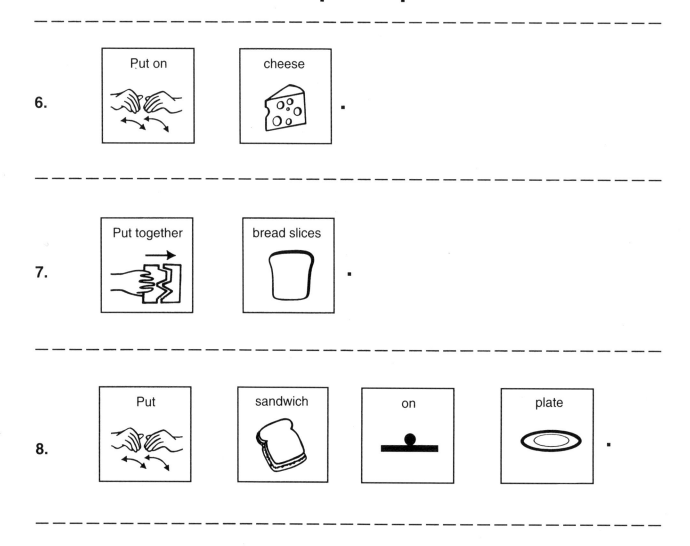

6. Put on cheese.

7. Put together bread slices.

8. Put sandwich on plate.

1. Duplicate recipe strips.
2. Cut along dotted lines.
3. Assemble in correct sequence.
4. Use during cooking activity/read symbol sentences.
5. Assemble into booklet form and bind left edge with staples if desired.

The Pigs' Picnic
Mr. Pig's Picnic Lunch

I eat | on a | picnic .

The Pigs' Picnic

Mr. Pig's Picnic Lunch

sandwich

apple

cookies

chips

soda

1. Identify, color, and cut out the above pictures.
2. Using gluesticks, paste these onto the picnic cloth on page 353.
3. As each food item is pasted on, read the symbol sentences together.

The Pigs' Picnic
What goes in the picnic basket?

Draw a line from the appropriate items to the picnic
basket and read the symbol sentences together.

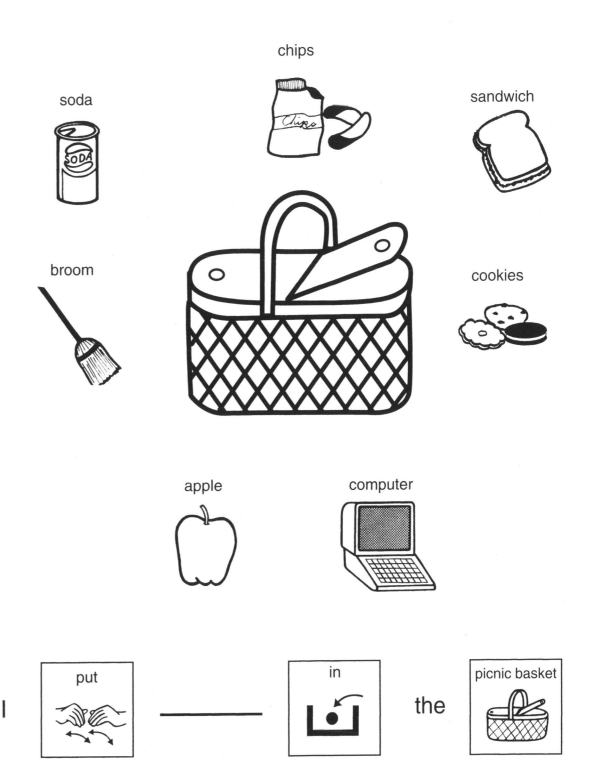

chips

soda

sandwich

broom

cookies

apple

computer

	put		in	the	picnic basket
I					.

The Pigs' Picnic
What Will Mr. Pig Wear?

The Pigs' Picnic
Tell Me About It!

1. Who was going on a picnic?

 dog
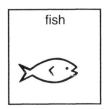 fish
 Mr. Pig
 cat

- -

2. Who did Mr. Pig meet on his way to the picnic?

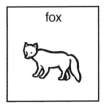 fox
 zebra
 boy
 lion

- -

3. What did his friends give him?

 hair
 money
 tail
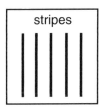 stripes

- -

4. Miss Pig thought he looked like a . . .

 dinosaur
 king
 snake
 monster

- -

1. Cut out into strips if desired.
2. Children can point to or mark correct answer.

Mr. Plg's Picnic Outfit

Draw a line from each of Mr. Pig's friends to the item that friend gave.

fox

hair

lion

stripes

zebra

tail

Resources and Literature List

Book Resources

Scholastic Inc.

(K-8 Catalog 1995)
P.O. Box 7502
Jefferson City, MO 65102
1-800-325-6149 • FAX: 1-800-560-6815

- *Big Pumpkin* by Erica Silverman

- *The Gingerbread Man* by Karen Schmidt

- **Chicken Soup With Rice* by Maurice Sendak

- **The Snowy Day* by Ezra Jack Keats

- **The Carrot Seed* by Ruth Krauss

- *More, More, More, Said the Baby* by Vera B. Williams

- **Goodnight Moon* by Margaret Wise Brown

- **Clean House for Mole and Mouse* by Harriet Ziefert

Demco

P.O. Box 7488
Madison, WI 53707-7488
1-800-356-1200 • FAX: 1-800-245-1329
or
P.O. Box 7767
Fresno, CA 93747

- *Goodnight Moon* by Margaret Wise Brown

- *The Snowy Day* by Ezra Jack Keats

SRA

MacGraw-Hill
P.O. Box 543
Blacklick, Ohio 43004
1-800-843-8855

- *The Pig's Picnic* by Keiko Kasza

* Big Books

Kaplan School Supply Corporation

1310 Lewisville-Clemmons Road • P.O. Box 609
Lewisville, N.C. 27023-609
1-336-766-7374 • 1-800-334-2014 • FAX: 336-766-5652

- ♦ *Are You My Mother* by P.D. Eastman

- ♦ *Goodnight Moon* by Margaret Wise Brown

- ♦ *The Snowy Day* by Ezra Jack Keats

- ♦ *The Carrot Seed* by Ruth Draus

- ♦ *The Gingerbread Man* traditional

Music:

- ♦ Raffi: *Singable Song for the Very Young, More Singable Songs for the Very Young, The Corner Grocery Store, Everything Grows, Raffi's Christmas Album*

- ♦ Kimbo Records: *Halloween Fun, Lullaby Time for Little People*

- ♦ Hap Palmer: *Learning Basic Skills Through Music: Vocabulary, Learning Basic Skills Through Music: Vol.-5 Witches Brew, Holiday Songs and Rhythms, Classic Nursery Rhymes*

- ♦ Greg & Steve: *We All Live Together Vol. 1-4*

BRODART BOOKS & SERVICES

500 Arch Street
Williamsport, PA 17701
1-717-326-2461 • 1-800-233-8467 • FAX: 800-999-6799

- ♦ *Gingerbread Boy* by Paul Galdone

- ♦ *Chicken Soup With Rice* by Maurice Sendak

- ♦ *The Snowy Day* by Ezra Jack Keats

- ♦ *Something Is Going to Happen* by Charlotte Zolotow

- ♦ *Are You My Mother?* by P.D. Eastman

- ♦ *Goodnight Moon* by Margaret Wise Brown

- ♦ *More, More, More, Said the Baby* by Vera B. Williams

- ♦ *Over the River and Through the Wood* by Lydia Maria Francis Child

Additional Resources

Resource Books:

Hands-on Reading by Jane Kelly and Teresa Friend

Engineering the Preschool Environment for Interactive, Symbolic Communication by Goossens', Crain, & Elder

Communication Displays for Engineered Preschool Environments: Book I and II by Goossens', Crain, & Elder

Total Augmentative Communication in the Early Childhood Classroom by Linda Burkhart

Units by Dianne DeTommaso

Quick Tech Readable, Repeatable Stories and Activities by Peggi McNairn and Cindy Shioleno

RAPS - Reading Activities Project for Older Students by Southwest Human Development Inc., Editor: Caroline Musselwhite

Storytime, Storytime Just For Fun, Storytime Holiday Fun by Patti King-DeBaun

AC System Vendors:

ADAMLAB
55 East Long Lake Rd. Suite 337
Troy, MI 48085
Phone: (248) 362-9603

Wolf, Hawk, AIPS Wolf, Wolf
cartridges

ZYGO
P.O. Box 1008, Portland, OR 97207-1008
Phone (800) 234-6006 • FAX: (503) 684-6011

Macaw

Ablenet
2808 Fairview Ave. N.
Roseville, MN 55113
Phone: (651) 294-2200 • FAX (651) 294-2259

Big Mac, switches, battery device
adapter, switch toys, Speakeasy
Environmental Control

Toys for Special Children
385 Warburton Ave., Hastings-on-Hudson, NY 10706
Phone (914) 478-0960

Cheap Talk, Talking Switch Plates
Switch Toys, Switches, Battery Device
Adapter, Environmental Control

Mayer-Johnson LLC
P.O. Box 1579, Solana Beach, CA 92075-1579
Phone (858) 550-0084 • FAX (858) 550-0449

Boardmaker, Speaking Dynamically

Software:

Laureate Learning Systems, Inc.
110 East Spring Street
Winooski, VT 05404
(800) 562-6801 • Fax (802) 655-4757

Edmark
222 Third Ave. SE 4th Floor
Cedar Rapids, IA 52401
Phone: 1-800-242-6747

Educational Resources
1550 Executive Dr.
P.O. Box 1900
Elgin, IL 60121-1900

Literature List

Holiday Fun Unit:

Big Pumpkin
    Erica Silverman

Macmillan Publishing Co..
New York, NY
    ISBN: 0-68-980129-7

Over the River and Through the Wood
    Lydia Maria Child

Harper Collins
New York, NY
    ISBN: 0-06-02130-5-5

Corduroy's Christmas
    Don Freeman

    ISBN: 0-67-084477-2

The Gingerbread Man
    Traditional

Scholastic, Inc.
New York, NY
    ISBN: 0-590-41056-3

The Easter Parade
    Mary Chalmers

Harper and Row
New York, NY
    ISBN: 0-06-021232-2

Family Fun Unit:

All by Myself
    Mercer Mayer (1983)

A Golden Book
Western Publishing Co.
Racine, Wisconsin, 53404
    ISBN: 0-307-11938-6
    ISBN: 0-307-61938-9 (lib. bdg.)

Are You My Mother?
    P. D. Eastman (1960)

Beginner Books
Random House
    ISBN: 0-688-09173-3
    ISBN: 0-688-09174-1 (lib. bdg.)

More, More, More, Said the Baby
    Vera B. Williams (1990)

E.P. Dutton
2 Park Avenue
New York, NY 10016
    ISBN: 0-14-050810-4

Don't Wake Up Mama!
    Eileen Christelow (1992)

Clarion Books
A Houghton Mifflin Co.
215 Park Ave. South
New York, NY
    ISBN: 0-395-60176-

Clean House for Mole and Mouse*
Harriet Ziefert (1988)

Puffin Books
Viking Penguin, Inc.
40 West 23rd Street
New York, NY 10003
ISBN: 0-14-050810-4

Goodnight Moon*
Margaret Wise Brown (1947)

HarperTrophy
A Division of HarperCollins
Harper & Row Publishers, Inc.
ISBN: 0-06-443017-0 (pbk)

Seasons of the Year Unit:

Chicken Soup With Rice
Maurice Sendak

Harper and Row
New York, NY
ISBN: 0-59071789-8

The Snowy Day
Ezra Jack Keats

The Viking Press
New York, NY
ISBN: 0-590-73323-0

Something Is Going to Happen
Charlotte Zolotow

Harper and Row
New York, NY
ISBN: 06-027028-4

The Carrot Seed
Ruth Krauss

Harper and Row
New York, NY
ISBN: 0-06443210-6

The Pigs' Picnic
Keiko Kasza

G.P. Putnam's Sons
New York, NY
ISBN: 0-399-21543-3

* Big Book

HANDS-ON READING

If you have enjoyed *More Hands-on Reading*, don't forget to purchase the original "Hands-on" book, *Hands-on Reading*. It has over 400 pages of fun-filled activities that go with popular children's books which can be found in most libraries. The two of these books, *More Hands-on Reading* and *Hands-on Reading* are a valuable resource for parents and teachers.

THE *PICTURE COMMUNICATION SYMBOLS BOOKS & PROGRAMS*

COMPUTER PROGRAMS
The PCS are available on computer discs for Apple, Macintosh®, and PC computers. Ideal for making communication boards and your own instructional materials. Several of the software versions allow translation into as many as ten languages. Call and request a catalog for more information.

STAMPS AND STICKERS
The PCS come available on both a stamp and sticker format, color-coded or black and white.

INSTRUCTIONAL MATERIALS AVAILABLE USING
THE *PICTURE COMMUNICATION SYMBOLS*

THIS IS THE ONE I WANT
A 172 page fun, color, cut, and paste activity book designed for the nonspeech or limited speech student. Thirty-four activities with accompanying question sheets and communication boards give many opportunities for symbol communication. May be easily adapted so that the instructor does the actual cutting and pasting for the physically handicapped client.

ENGINEERING THE PRESCHOOL ENVIRONMENT FOR SYMBOLIC COMMUNICATION
An exceptional 200 page practical guide covering all aspects of preschool methods, ideas, resources, etc. Specifics are given for such things as designing core and supplemental displays, how to make an eye-point horseshoe display, an eye-point vest and rotary scanner display. With a wealth of other practical information, this book should prove to be a valuable resource for all persons working in the AAC field.

COMMUNICATION DISPLAYS FOR ENGINEERED PRESCHOOL ENVIRONMENTS, BOOKS I AND II
Collectively, Displays Books I and II provide a total of 396 communication displays designed for the preschool environment. The displays in Books I and II are based on the same 100 activities but are laid out in different configurations.

TOTAL AUGMENTATIVE COMMUNICATION IN THE EARLY CHILDHOOD CLASSROOM
A 248 page comprehensive guide to augmentative communication and technology. The book is full of practical ideas and information. Topics covered include manual communication boards, sign language, facilitated communication, powered mobility, voice-output, picture and symbol systems, emergent literacy skills, emergent math, objectives and evaluation of performance, teaching techniques, instructional materials strategies, and an extensive list of resources. This is an exceptional book including many illustrations and examples.

UNITS

Units is a 208 page book consisting of 9 units for preschool and elementary classrooms. Individual unit titles are Shapes, My Body, Indian, Winter Fun, Alphabet, Animals, Community Workers, Earth, and Transportation. Each unit has lessons in art, music, cooking, and literacy. Communication overlays, in two sizes, are also provided in two configurations (9 and 36 cell). The displays may be used separately or on the Wolf. A Wolf Cap will also be available for the book.

LISTEN TO THIS!

This 290 page book is full of reproducible auditory processing exercises designed for low-level clients. It is designed for both non-speaking and speaking clients of any age. No reading is required by the client to successfully complete the exercises. The client is provided with repetitive practice in the five areas of categorization, word retrieval, auditory association, problem solving, and auditory memory.

STORIES ABOUT ME!

Here's a chance for clients of all ages to "write" and "read" stories about themselves. Each story is four or five lines long and is made primarily with the Picture Communication Symbols. The client fills in the blanks to personalize each story. Over 200 reproducible stories are designed around home and family, school, activities, sports, holidays, weather and health and augmentative aids. A great way to encourage language with clients who have limited expressive language abilities.

SIMPLY SILLY ABOUT SENTENCES

Let Silly Sue, Maxi the Dog, and the DoRight Twins lead you through 280 pages of reproducible low-level language exercises. The exercises are designed for clients of all ages who need repetitive practice expressing three and four word sentence structures. The program focuses on five main topic areas: Grooming, Meals, Body Parts, Clothing, and Chores.

EVERYBODY'S DOING IT!

A 440 page source book of full-bodied action pictures for teaching the use of verbs. 55 verbs are targeted in 527 different situations. Each character in the picture may be customized for hair and clothing.

INTRODUCTION TO KITCHEN APPLIANCES

The *Introduction to Kitchen Appliances* is a 144 page workbook designed for teaching the use of appliances in a home or school situation. Emphasis is placed on the function and safety of individual appliances. The appliances covered in the lessons are: the stove, oven, freezer, microwave, and refrigerator.

HEALTH UNITS FOR NONREADERS

Health Units for Non-Readers is a 148 page reproducible workbook for helping teach good health habits and personal grooming. The workbook is designed for use with individuals or small groups and consists of short picture symbol stories and activities. The materials provide a good supplement to basic education, independent living, and communication classes.

STORYTIME

Are you looking for a book with beginning literacy activities for young special needs children? *Storytime* has 181 pages of entertaining and interactive stories combined with suggested related literacy activities. Included are activity ideas for art, writing, play, and cooking. A language board is included with each lesson as well as instructions on how to adapt the lessons for physically challenged students.

STORYTIME - JUST FOR FUN

The follow up book to the entertaining and interactive stories of *Storytime Tales*. *Storytime - Just For Fun* has 244 pages containing 5 new stories, symbols, and emergent literacy activities.

WHAT'S IN YOUR HOME?
WHAT'S IN YOUR COMMUNITY?

Low-level workbooks that each student may keep as their own. The books are designed for students who need practice with everyday vocabulary, such as "chair", "store", and "bedroom". Each workbook includes discussion sheets, study sheets, vocabulary worksheets, unit reviews, and unit review worksheets.

LIFE EXPERIENCES KIT
A unique set of eleven different "lesson plans" designed for non-speech or limited speech students. The plans and materials teach specific daily life activity skills, such as "Make Juice," "Wash Hands," and "Go Restaurant." Included are symbol instruction sheets and communication boards.

PICTURE SYMBOL LOTTO
This special lotto game is set up in color coded sections of verbs, adjectives, and nouns. An excellent opportunity to reinforce common vocabulary and color-coding cues used on communication boards.

HOLIDAY KIT
The Holiday Kit is a set of low level materials based on holidays designed to stimulate enthusiasm, interest, and conversation in your clients. The kit includes a folder and 9 pre-made communication boards in both 1" and 2" sizes. Symbol masters for an additional 15 holidays are also included.

ZOO KIT
The Zoo Kit is a companion to the Food Kit or it may be used separately. It expands symbol reading and sentence building skills so that the symbol users may create their own story. It includes worksheets, stamps, and lesson plans with the zoo and animals as the topic.

QUICK TECH MAGIC: MUSIC BASED ACTIVITIES
Music based literacy activities for the elementary-aged child. This 232 page book includes a CD of delightful tunes. Each song has a music score, language and literacy activities, and recommended adaptations for students with special needs. Music can be a magical vehicle towards the enhancement of literacy.

I CAN COOK, TOO!
A wonderful book that is filled with kid-tested recipes suitable for children with and without special needs. In addition to recipes, each topic has communication overlays and carryover activities. Chapters are set up according to months and seasonal holidays — enough activities to keep the class busy for an entire school year.

THE PRESCHOOL AAC CHECKLIST (3 COPIES) AND VIDEO
The checklists are 116 page booklets for teacher guidance and for tracking students' progress in augmentative communication. The booklets also contain symbols and student remediation materials. A 20 minute video provides a good introduction.

WHO, WHAT AND WHY
A unique set of activities and worksheets help students understand and differentiate between "wh" questions and answers.

PLAYTIME
An excellent resource to help parents, teachers, and therapists teach vocabulary through games and poems.

SOCIAL SKILLS STORIES
A 400 page book filled with interesting characters in stories that walk them through a variety of social situations including gift giving, social proximity, saying thank you, appropriate comments, etc. A terrific resource.

For further information on these products and others, please call or write for our free brochure.

Mayer-Johnson LLC
P.O. Box 1579
Solana Beach, CA 92075-7579
U.S.A.
Phone (858) 550-0084 or (800) 588-4548
Fax (858) 550-0449